CÉDRIC

Gevaarlijk transport

Scenario en tekeningen: LAUDEC

Inkleuring: LEONARDO

DUPUIS

Voor mijn vriend Raoul.

Laudec

Cédric is een reeks die werd bedacht
door Cauvin en Laudec.

Eerste druk

ISBN: 978-90-314-4166-2
Wettelijk depot: D/2024/0089/174

Vertaling: the house of BOOM!, Wingene
Lettering: LaGrafica

Gedrukt in de EU door Rotolito.
www.dupuis.com

Rijles
TING TING
?
CÉDRIC, WAT DOE JE DAAR? KUN JE WEL MET DIE STEP RIJDEN?
JA, OPA. NICO HEEFT 'T ME GELEERD.
DIE STEP HERINNERT ME AAN M'N JEUGD. DAT WAS 'N ZALIGE TIJD. (ZUCHT)
WAREN ER AL STEPS TOEN U KIND WAS?
HAHAHA!
WAT DACHT JE, JONGEN? DAT DE WERELD PAS IS BEGINNEN TE DRAAIEN TOEN JIJ GEBOREN WERD? IK WAS OP JOUW LEEFTIJD AL DE KAMPIOEN VAN ONS DORP.
ZAL IK JE EEN DEMONSTRATIE GEVEN? DAN ZIE JE 'T MET JE EIGEN OGEN.
EH... WEES WEL VOORZICHTIG, MENEER. DIT IS EEN ELEKTRISCHE STEP MET 'N OPGEDREVEN MOTOR. IK WEET NIET OF U...
ACH, HET IS ZOALS MET FIETSEN, JONGEN. ALS JE 'T ONDER DE KNIE HEBT, VERLEER JE HET NOOIT MEER.
WAT EEN GROTE STEP, ZEG. WE KUNNEN ER ZELFS MET Z'N VIEREN OP.
MAAL... IS DAT WEL VOOLZICHTIG, MENEEL?
JA HOOR. WEES MAAR NIET BANG. IK RIJD NIET VER.
HOU JULLIE GOED VAST. IEDEREEN KLAAR?
506/1

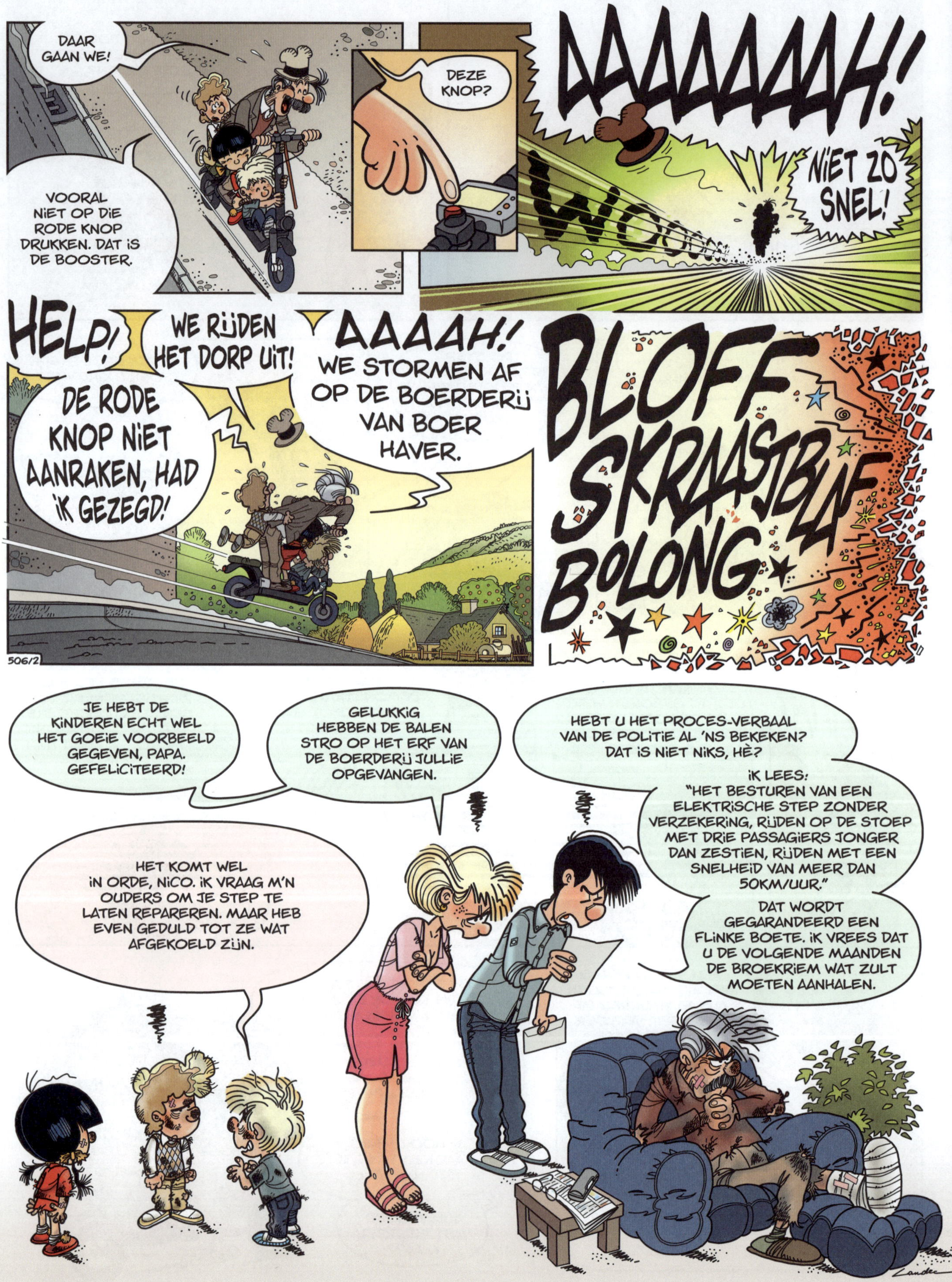

DAAR GAAN WE!
VOORAL NIET OP DIE RODE KNOP DRUKKEN. DAT IS DE BOOSTER.
DEZE KNOP?
DAAAAAAAH!
WOOO...
NIET ZO SNEL!
HELP!
WE RIJDEN HET DORP UIT!
DE RODE KNOP NIET AANRAKEN, HAD IK GEZEGD!
AAAAH! WE STORMEN AF OP DE BOERDERIJ VAN BOER HAVER.
BLOFF SKRAASJBLAF BOLONG
506/2
JE HEBT DE KINDEREN ECHT WEL HET GOEIE VOORBEELD GEGEVEN, PAPA. GEFELICITEERD!
GELUKKIG HEBBEN DE BALEN STRO OP HET ERF VAN DE BOERDERIJ JULLIE OPGEVANGEN.
HEBT U HET PROCES-VERBAAL VAN DE POLITIE AL 'NS BEKEKEN? DAT IS NIET NIKS, HÈ?
IK LEES: "HET BESTUREN VAN EEN ELEKTRISCHE STEP ZONDER VERZEKERING, RIJDEN OP DE STOEP MET DRIE PASSAGIERS JONGER DAN ZESTIEN, RIJDEN MET EEN SNELHEID VAN MEER DAN 50KM/UUR."
DAT WORDT GEGARANDEERD EEN FLINKE BOETE. IK VREES DAT U DE VOLGENDE MAANDEN DE BROEKRIEM WAT ZULT MOETEN AANHALEN.
HET KOMT WEL IN ORDE, NICO. IK VRAAG M'N OUDERS OM JE STEP TE LATEN REPAREREN. MAAR HEB EVEN GEDULD TOT ZE WAT AFGEKOELD ZIJN.

Uitstel van executie

Smullen maar!

AAN TAFEL! EEN ERG BIJZONDER GERECHT, VANAVOND. WE BEGINNEN MET SOEP VAN AARDAPPELSCHILLEN, RADIJSJES, GROEN VAN WORTELEN, LENTE-UITJES, PAARDENBLOEMEN, STUKJES KOOL, BROODKORSTEN EN ZWOERD.
DAARNA HEB IK LASAGNE VAN BIETBLAADJES, SPINAZIE MET BÉCHAMELSAUS, MAÏS EN PESTO MET DASLOOK.
EN ALS DESSERT KRIJGEN JULLIE CAKE VAN BANANENSCHILLEN, RABARBERBLAADJES EN MAGERE YOGHURT. SMAKELIJK!
HEE, WAAR GAAN JULLIE NAARTOE?
NOG DRIE BAKJES FRIET, ALSJEBLIEFT!
MET VEEL MAYONAISE.
EN KETCHUP!
KOMT ERAAN!
FRIETEN KOX
492/2
Laudec

'n Verkeerd adres

* ZIE ALBUM 25.

iK HEB EEN ANDER iDEE.
OEi! DAT BELOOFT!
GA NAAR HUiS EN SCHRiJF EEN BRiEFJE VOOR CHEN. WE ZiEN ELKAAR MORGEN HiER.
DE VOLGENDE DAG.
KiJK!
EEN DRONE?
NiET ZOMAAR EEN DRONE. DE VADER VAN NiCO HEEFT 'M MEEGEBRACHT VAN EEN REiS NAAR AZiË.
DAAR WORDEN DRONES GEBRUiKT OM POST EN PAKJES TE BEZORGEN.
iK MOEST AANDRiNGEN, MAAR JE MAG 'M ENKELE UREN LENEN.
DE MEiSJES STAAN BiJ DE FONTEiN. WE STUREN DE DRONE DiE KANT UiT, LATEN 'M EVEN ZAKKEN ALS HiJ BOVEN CHEN HANGT EN LOSSEN DAN HET BRiEFJE.
500/2
HOP, DAAR GAAT HiJ!
ZZZZZZZZZZZZZZRRRRRRR

DIT IS HET IDEALE MOMENT. CHEN STAAT WAT APART. IK LAAT DE DRONE ZAKKEN.
FLAP FLAP FLAP
FLAP FLAP FLAP
ZZZZZZZZZZZZZZZZZZZZZZZ
OEI! DE DRONE ZAL... HIJ BLIJFT IN DE BOOM HANGEN!
500/3
IK... IK BEN DE CONTROLE KWIJT!
ZZKPFZZZKRAAK
DE ENVELOP IS GEVALLEN!

?
Ik ben verliefd op je sinds de allereerste dag. Jij bent het mooiste meisje van de school en ik wil later met je trouwen.
Cédric♡
?? ?
?
CÉDRIC? CÉDRIC, WAAR BEN JE?
?
CÉDRiiiiiiC?....
CÉDRIC?....
TOK TOK
KOM ER MAAR UIT. ZE IS WEG.
CÉDRIC?
WEER MISLUKT! IK ZEI TOCH DAT HET NIKS ZOU WORDEN.
WAAROM WORD JE NIET OP EEN ANDER MEISJE VERLIEFD? M'N ZUS ADELINE BIJVOORBEELD. ZE ZIET JE GRAAG, DAT WEET JE. ZE HOOPT AL LANG DAT JE CHEN UIT JE HOOFD ZET.
IK WIL JE ZUS NIET, STOMKOP! IK WIL CHEN!
500/4

Onzekere toekomst

CHEN WORDT ERG VERWEND. ZE GAAN VAAK UIT ETEN EN GEREGELD MET VAKANTIE.
NICO MAAKT MEER KANS OM MET HAAR TE TROUWEN DAN JIJ. ALS JE DAT MAAR WEET!
NICO?
UITERAARD. ZIJN VADER IS DIPLOMAAT. HIJ VLIEGT HET HELE JAAR LANG ROND MET PRIVÉVLIEGTUIGEN EN HIJ KAN Z'N FAMILIE MEENEMEN OVER DE HELE WERELD. BOVENDIEN WORDT HIJ VAAK UITGENODIGD OP BELANGRIJKE AVONDEN EN DURE FEESTJES. DAN MOGEN ZE OOK MEE.
JOUW VADER VERKOOPT TAPIJTEN, JE MOEDER WERKT BIJ EEN BAKKER EN JE OPA LEGDE TREINSPOREN. DAAR MAAK JE WEINIG INDRUK MEE.
502/2
BLAM
OEI! IS ER WAT, CÉDRIC? JE ZIET ER ZO ONGELUKKIG UIT, JONGEN?
ALS CHEN LATER MET NICO TROUWT, IS DAT JULLIE SCHULD!

Huwelijksverjaardag

KOM EVEN, KNUL. IK ZAL JE EEN VERHAALTJE VERTELLEN.
JE OMA EN IK HEBBEN ONZE HUWELIJKS-VERJAARDAG OOK ALTIJD ALLEEN GEVIERD.
WIJ HADDEN HET GELD NIET OM NAAR EEN RESTAURANT TE GAAN. WE GINGEN DANSEN IN EEN ZAALTJE BIJ HET WATER AAN DE RAND VAN HET DORP. HET WAS ONZE ENIGE UITSTAP VAN HET JAAR.
KROON
ONDERTUSSEN PASTE M'N NICHT ERNESTINE THUIS OP JE MOEDER.
WEET JE DAT NOG, MARIE-ROSE?
NEE. DAAR WAS IK VEEL TE KLEIN VOOR.
496/2

TOT...
JOOST, GERMAINE... WACHT EVEN! MARIE-ROSE VOELT ZICH NIET LEKKER.
TOEN IK HAAR IN BED WILDE LEGGEN, GLOEIDE HAAR VOORHOOFD. IK BEN BANG DAT ZE KOORTS HEEFT.
EN NIET VEEL LATER.
GA JIJ MAAR NAAR HUIS, ERNESTINE. WIJ ZORGEN VOOR MARIE-ROSE.
EH... WEET JE 'T ZEKER?
TRRR TRRR TRRR TRRR TRRR TRRR
KUNT U SNEL KOMEN, DOKTER? MARIE-ROSE HEEFT HOGE KOORTS... GOED, WE WACHTEN OP U.
EN...
TOK TOK TOK
DAG, JOOST. WAAR IS DE ZIEKE?
IN HAAR KAMER BOVEN, DOKTER. MIJN VROUW IS BIJ HAAR.
HET IS NIET ERNSTIG. GEEF HAAR OM DE TWEE UUR TIEN DRUPPELS EN LEG EEN VOCHTIGE DOEK OP HAAR VOORHOOFD.
496/3
WE HEBBEN TOEN UREN AAN HAAR BED GEZETEN. WE VERTELDEN VERHAALTJES EN MOPPEN, IN DE HOOP HAAR WAT OP TE MONTEREN.

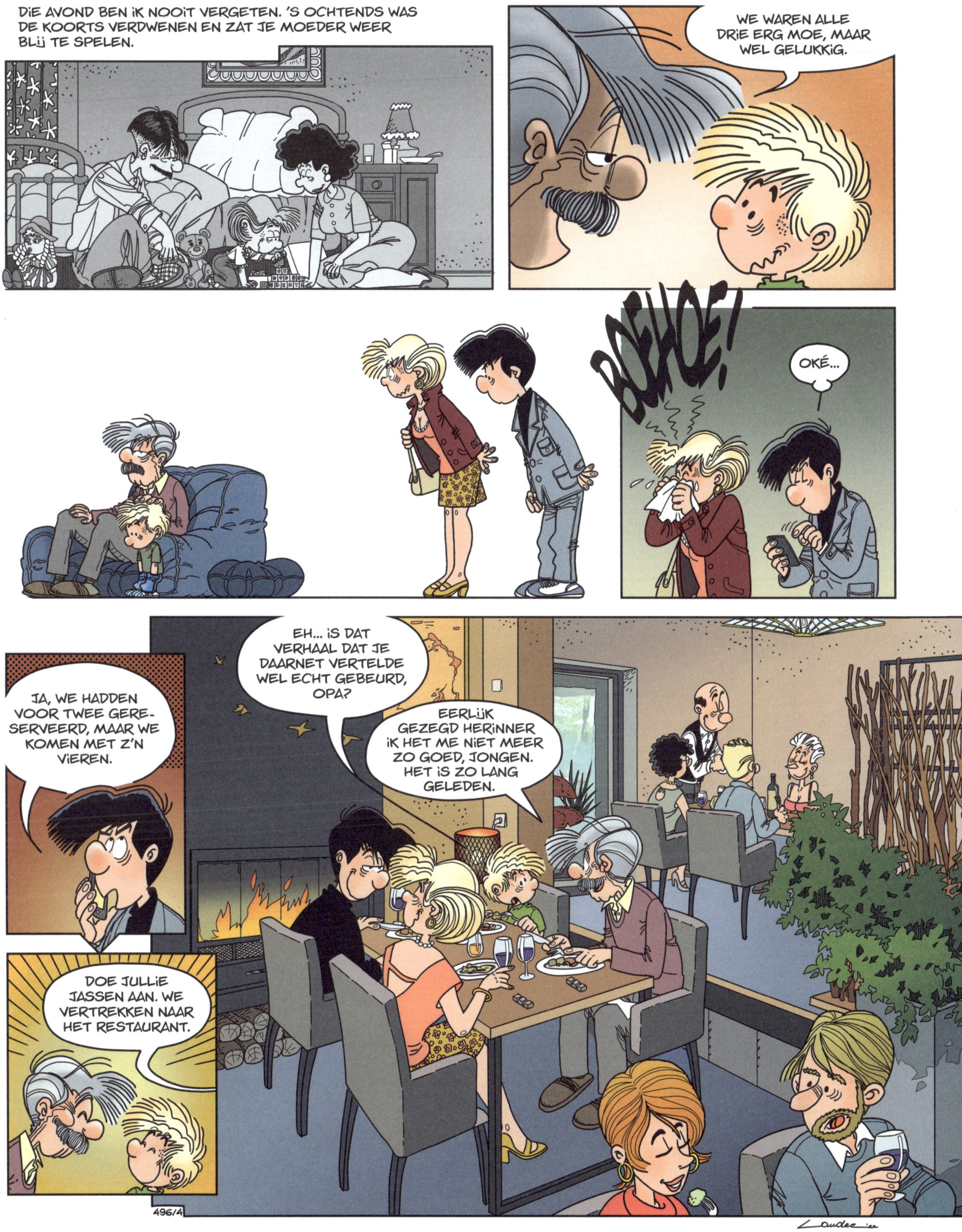
DIE AVOND BEN IK NOOIT VERGETEN. 'S OCHTENDS WAS DE KOORTS VERDWENEN EN ZAT JE MOEDER WEER BLIJ TE SPELEN.
WE WAREN ALLE DRIE ERG MOE, MAAR WEL GELUKKIG.
BOEHOE!
OKÉ...
JA, WE HADDEN VOOR TWEE GERE-SERVEERD, MAAR WE KOMEN MET Z'N VIEREN.
DOE JULLIE JASSEN AAN. WE VERTREKKEN NAAR HET RESTAURANT.
EH... IS DAT VERHAAL DAT JE DAARNET VERTELDE WEL ECHT GEBEURD, OPA?
EERLIJK GEZEGD HERINNER IK HET ME NIET MEER ZO GOED, JONGEN. HET IS ZO LANG GELEDEN.
496/4

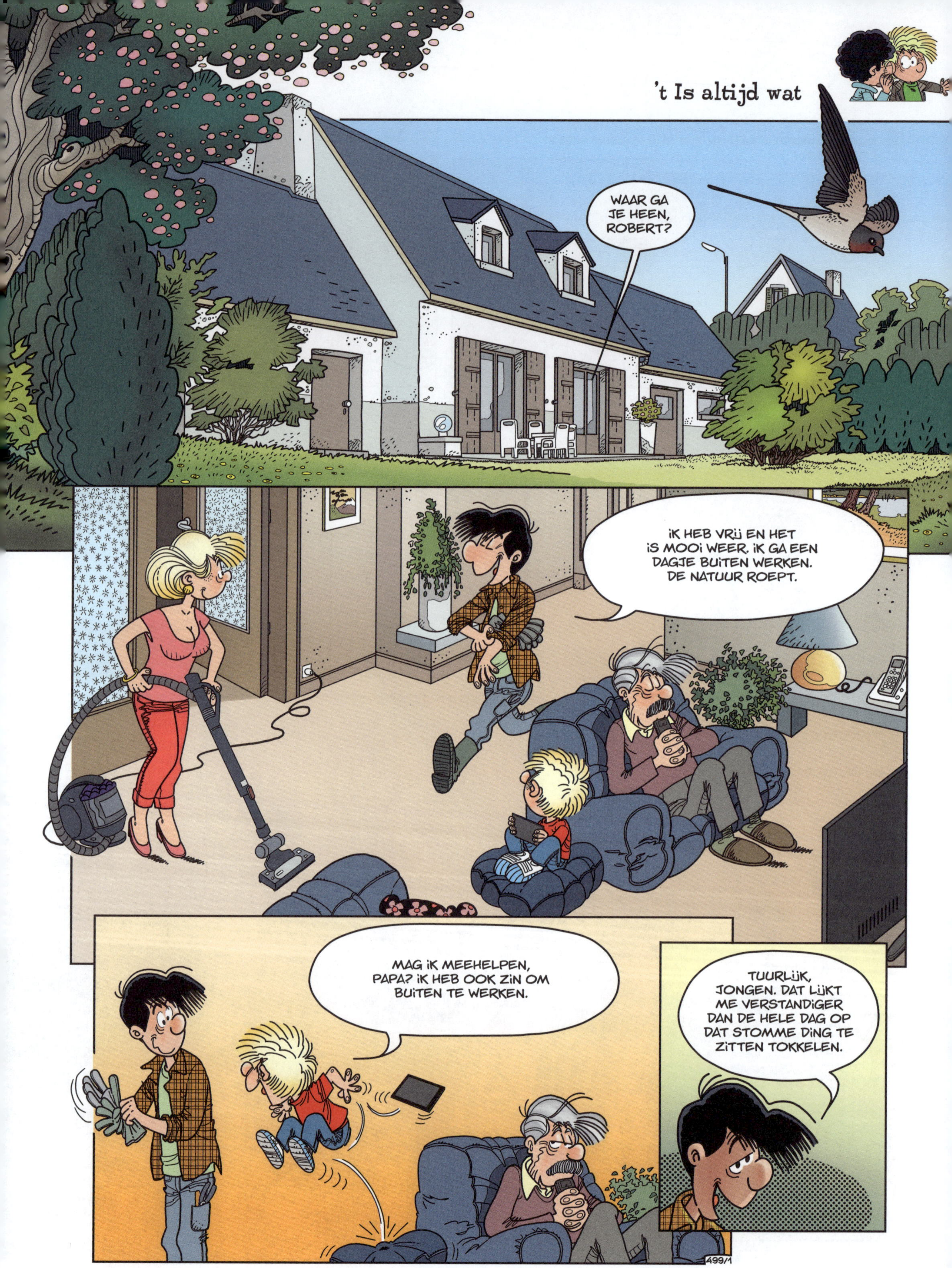
WAAR GA JE HEEN, ROBERT?
IK HEB VRIJ EN HET IS MOOI WEER. IK GA EEN DAGJE BUITEN WERKEN. DE NATUUR ROEPT.
MAG IK MEEHELPEN, PAPA? IK HEB OOK ZIN OM BUITEN TE WERKEN.
TUURLIJK, JONGEN. DAT LIJKT ME VERSTANDIGER DAN DE HELE DAG OP DAT STOMME DING TE ZITTEN TOKKELEN.
499/1

U BLIJFT WAARSCHIJNLIJK LIEVER IN UW LUIE STOEL NAAR DE TV GAPEN, SCHOONPAPA?
GRMMMBL...
KLIK
...IS DE NATUUR DIT JAAR DE AFGELOPEN MAANDEN BLIJKBAAR HEEL ERG ONVOORSPELBAAR.
?
HET NOORDEN VAN HET LAND WORDT GEPLAAGD DOOR HEVIGE REGENBUIEN WAARDOOR HEEL WAT BEKEN EN RIVIERTJES BUITEN HUN OEVERS ZIJN GETREDEN. MET ALS GEVOLG NOOIT EERDER GEZIENE OVERSTROMINGEN.
IN HET WESTEN DEED EEN AARDBEVING MET EEN KRACHT VAN DRIE OP DE SCHAAL VAN RICHTER EEN AANTAL RUITEN EN HEEL WAT SCHOORSTENEN SNEUVELEN. GELUKKIG WERD DAARBIJ NIEMAND GEWOND.
NIKS AAN TE DOEN, DE MOTOR WIL NIET STARTEN. HET IS TE VOCHTIG.
DAT VALT TEGEN, HÈ?! HOE GA JE NU HET GRAS MAAIEN?
BLUBRRRPRUT BLUB
ALS DIT NOG LANG DUURT, KAN IK VANDAAG M'N REKENINGEN NIET MEER AFSLUITEN.
IK KAN NIET SPELEN.
DE NATUUR HEEFT OOK HET ZUIDEN NIET GESPAARD. DAAR WOEDEN SINDS VANOCHTEND ENKELE HEVIGE BOSBRANDEN. DE BRANDWEER IS NAAR HEEL WAT PLEKKEN UITGERUKT.
PAPA, ER LIGT NOG WORST OP DE BARBECUE.
ZWIJG EN REN, JONGEN!
WEL, ROBERT? ROEPT DE NATUUR NIET MEER?
JE BENT NIET GRAPPIG, MARIE-ROSE!
Z Z Z Z Z Z Z Z Z
TUP TUP BLIB
BIPTUUUT
BIP BIP
BLIP
499/2

* SOCIAL MEDIAKANAAL VOOR KINDEREN.

ANGOULÊME 873 KM
IK HEB GEEN FOTO VAN CÉDRIC. IK ZOU NIET WETEN WAAR IK DIE MOET HALEN.
VRAAG HEM EEN FOTO ZONDER TE ZEGGEN WAT JE ERMEE GAAT DOEN.
DAT LUKT NOOIT. CÉDRIC IS ALTIJD VERSCHRIKKELIJK ACHTERDOCHTIG.
KUNNEN WE HET NIET PROBEREN?
DING DONG
DAG, MENEER. IS CÉDRIC THUIS?
NEE, HIJ IS ER NIET. KAN IK JULLIE ERGENS MEE HELPEN?
WEL, EH... U WEET WAARSCHIJNLIJK DAT CÉDRIC VERLIEFD IS OP CHEN.
Z'N VIETNAMESE VRIENDINNETJE. JA, NATUURLIJK!
ZE IS CHINESE.
NU JA, WAT MAAKT HET UIT. EN...?
COLINE IS EEN VRIENDIN VAN CHEN. ZE IS OOK BLOGGER EN INFLUENCER OP SOCIALE MEDIA.
WAT IS ZE?!
495/2

WEL, ZE SCHRIJFT BERICHTEN OP INTERNET. OP PAGINA'S DIE.... EH, HET IS VOOR MENSEN DIE... EH, HET IS EIGENLIJK TE INGEWIKKELD OM UIT TE LEGGEN.
JAJA. ZEG MAAR METEEN DAT IK TE OUD BEN OM HET TE SNAPPEN. TE OUD EN TE DOM.
EEN LANGE UITLEG LATER...
EN DAAROM WILLEN WE GRAAG EEN MOOIE FOTO VAN CÉDRIC.
EEN MOOIE FOTO?
KOM MAAR. IK WEET PRECIES WAT JULLIE NODIG HEBBEN.
KIJK! DEZE KUN JE VAST GEBRUIKEN, NEE?
HET IS EEN FOTO WAAR HIJ ZELF ERG ENTHOUSIAST OVER IS.
DE... DENKT U DAT ECHT?
JA HOOR. HIJ ZAL VAST HEEL BLIJ ZIJN.
495/3
MAAR JE BRENGT DE FOTO DAARNA WEL WEER TERUG, HÈ.

DE VOLGENDE DAG.
DAG, CHEN. WAAR MOET IEDEREEN ZO OM LACHEN? WAT IS ER GEBEURD?
HALLO, CÉDLIC.
HAHAHA HOHO!
HAHAHA HA!
WOEHA HAHA!
HAHAHA!
!
HIHIHI!
HAHAHA!
HIHIHIHOHO HAHA!
HIHIHIHI! HAHAHA! HIHIHIHI!
HAHAHAHA HOHOHO!
JE ZIET EL HIELOP HEEL LIEF UIT!
LIEF? WAAR?
CHEN, voor altijd!
SAMZONG
DAAARGL... 'N RAMP!
WACHT, IK ZAL HET UIT-LEGGEN. COLINE WILDE JE HELPEN EN...
CHRISTIAN, KOM HIER! WIE HEEFT DIT GEDAAN? VAN WIE KREEG JE DIE FOTO?
495/4

Nooit opgeven

Herinneringen

OUD NIET, MAAR IK WIL GRAAG SNEL GROOT ZIJN OM MET CHEN TE KUNNEN TROUWEN.
TOEN IK JOUW LEEFTIJD HAD, VOND IK OOK DAT DE TIJD NIET SNEL GENOEG GING.
OP M'N ZEVENTIENDE GING IK VOOR DE SPOORWEGEN WERKEN EN LEERDE IK TREINSPOREN LEGGEN.
IK LEERDE OOK GERMAINE KENNEN... ZE WAS HET ALLER-MOOISTE MEISJE VAN HET DORP.
EVEN MOOI ALS CHEN?
VEEL MOOIER NOG.
DAT KAN NIET! CHEN IS HET MOOISTE MEISJE!
JA, GOED. LAAT ME VERDER VERTELLEN. WE MOCHTEN ELKAAR NOOIT ALLEEN ZIEN, DAT WAS ZO IN DIE TIJD. HAAR OUDERS HIELDEN ONS ALTIJD IN DE GATEN. DAAROM WILDEN WE ZO SNEL MOGELIJK TROUWEN.
IK WERKTE HEEL HARD, DEED ZOVEEL MOGELIJK OVERUREN EN PROBEERDE GOED TE SPAREN. GERMAINE NAAIDE EN VERSTELDE KLEREN VOOR MENSEN UIT DE BUURT.
SINGER
DE TIJD KNAAGDE LANGZAAM VERDER, MAAR UITEINDELIJK KONDEN WE ONZE DROOM WAARMAKEN. WE TROUWDEN, EN...
...KREGEN EEN WOLK VAN EEN BABY. WE KONDEN ONS GEEN MOOIER LEVEN VOORSTELLEN.
VREEMD GENOEG GING DE TIJD VANAF DAT MOMENT INEENS VEEL SNELLER. STEEDS SNELLER, EIGENLIJK, EN HET WAS ONMOGELIJK OM HEM EVEN STIL TE ZETTEN EN OP ADEM TE KOMEN.
503/2

TOEN KWAM DE DAG DAT GERMAINE NIET MEER VERDER KON EN DEFINITIEF AFHAAKTE. SINDSDIEN STA IK ER ALLEEN VOOR.
ER ZAT EEN STEENTJE IN HAAR SCHOEN, HÈ? ZO IS ZE TOCH GESTORVEN?
JA, EH... DAT IS DE MOOIE VERSIE. IK HEB JE 'T VERHAAL AL EERDER VERTELD.*
* ZIE ALBUM 5.
HOE OUDER IK WORD, HOE SNELLER DE TIJD LIJKT TE GAAN. VANDAAG VERTEL JIJ ME AL OVER JE HUWELIJK MET JE VIETNAMEESJE.
CHINESE!
GENIET NOG MAAR EVEN VAN JE LEVEN, KNUL. DOE DINGEN DIE KINDEREN VAN JOUW LEEFTIJD LEUK VINDEN.
CÉDRIC, GAUW! CHEN IS HELEMAAL ALLEEN BIJ DE VIJVER. JE KUNT NU RUSTIG MET HAAR PRATEN, ALS JE WILT.
IK PRAAT LATER WEL MET HAAR. KOM, NU GAAN WE VOETBALLEN.
O? ECHT?
503/3
GELIJK HEB JE. ZOLANG JE JONG BENT, MOET JE ERVAN GENIETEN.
JULLIE BESEFFEN HET NATUURLIJK NIET, MAAR DIT IS DE MOOISTE TIJD VAN JE LEVEN.

Een vrije dag

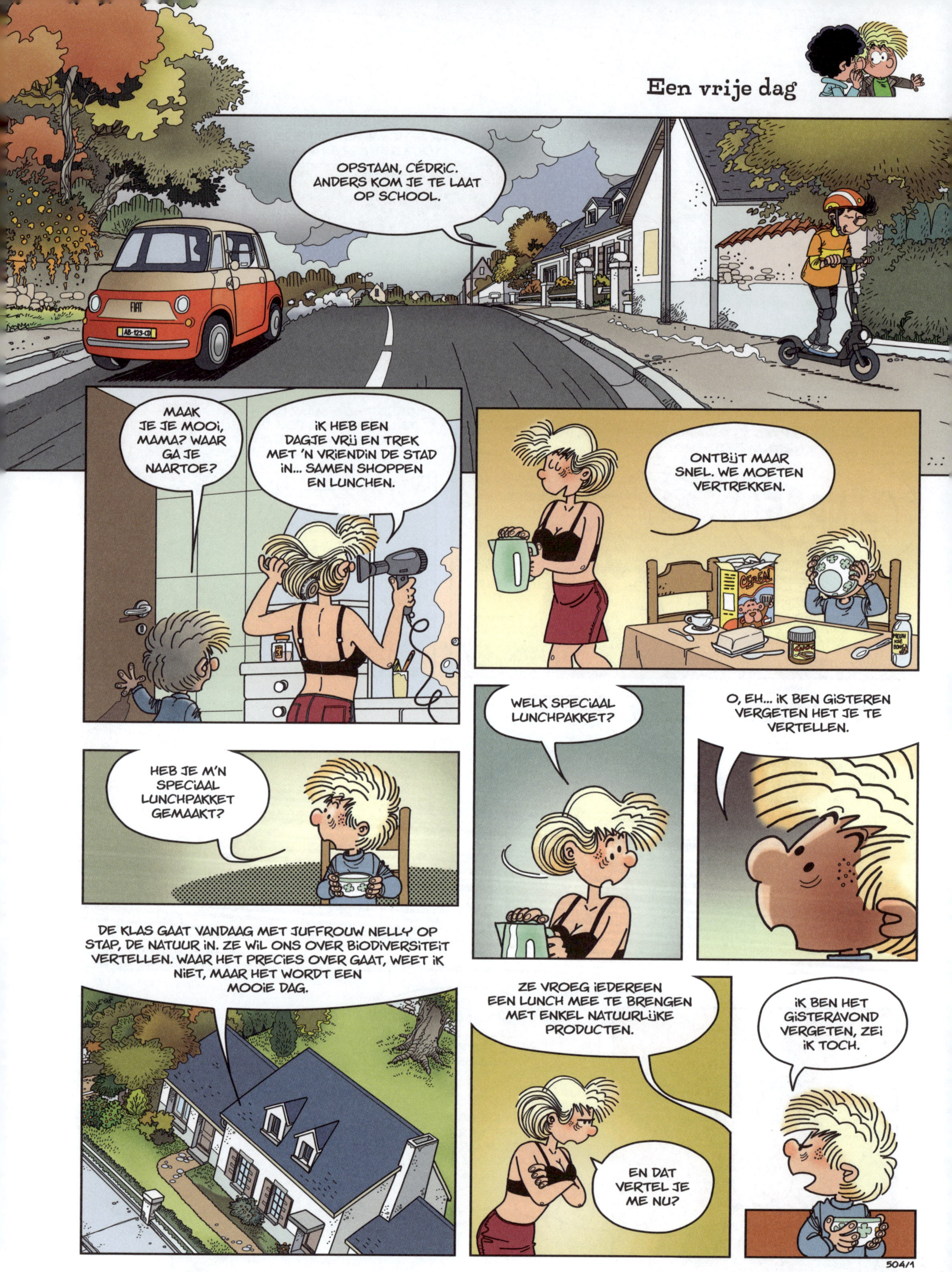

GOED DAN. KLEED JE AAN EN WACHT OP ME. IK LOOP SNEL NAAR DE KRUIDENIER.
WAT LATER.
PFT... IK WIST NIET DAT HET 'S OCHTENDS VROEG AL ZO DRUK WAS BIJ DE KRUIDENIER.
HAAST JE, MAMA. STRAKS KOM IK NOG TE LAAT OP SCHOOL.
ZO, 'N VRUCHTENSLAATJE MET VRUCHTEN UIT DE STREEK EN VOLKORENBROOD MET KAAS VAN BOER HAVER.
HAAST JE! HAAST JE!
TOT VANAVOND, MAMA. IK VERTREK.
HEE! EN JE LUNCH?
DAN ZEG JE: "DANK JE, MAMA!"
DANK JE, MAMA!
BLAM
MOOI! NU GA IK ME SNEL KLAARMAKEN.
IK KOM NOOIT OP TIJD!
BLAM
MARIE-ROSE!
ROBERT? BEN JIJ DAT?
504/2

KOM JE EVEN? IK HEB JE NODIG.
?
IK HEB STRAKS EEN ZAKENLUNCH MET EEN GROTE KLANT. ER HANGT EEN BELANGRIJK CONTRACT AAN VAST... VEEL GELD!
IK HEB EEN AFSPRAAK IN EEN STERRENRESTAURANT EN IK WIL ER GOED UITZIEN. PAK, DAS, EEN GESTREKEN HEMD.
JE BOFT. IK HEB GISTEREN JE HEMD VAN EGYPTISCH KATOEN GEWASSEN. IK STRIJK HET GAUW.
PSSS SJJJJ
WIL JE OOK NOG EVEN M'N ZWARTE SCHOENEN POETSEN, SCHAT? EN SNEL, ALSJEBLIEFT. DANK JE!
VAN EEN ONTSPANNENDE VRIJE DAG GESPROKEN.
FRRRT FRRRT
504/3

IK GA WEER. TOT STRAKJES.
DAN VERTEL IK JE OF DE LUNCH EEN SUCCES IS GEWEEST.
ROBERT, JE KOFFERTJE!
OEPS. DANK JE, SCHAT.
SMAK!
PFUUU! HOPELIJK KAN IK ME NU EINDELIJK ZELF KLAAR-MAKEN.
CIAO!
DAG...
ZEG, IK HAD VANOCHTEND EEN IDEE. IK HEB ER ZELF EERLIJK GEZEGD WEL ZIN IN.
?
JIJ BENT VANDAAG TOCH VRIJ, HÈ. ZULLEN WE SAMEN UITGEBREID LUNCHEN? MET GEBAKKEN EIEREN, SPEK, TOMAATJES IN DE OVEN, WORST, GEBAKKEN AARDAPPELEN... EN EEN GROOT GLAS VERSGEPERST VRUCHTENSAP.
WE HEBBEN TENSLOTTE DE HELE OCHTEND DE TIJD.
504/4
HEE, WAAR GA JE NAARTOE?
IK GA WERKEN.
MAAR... JE HAD TOCH EEN VRIJE DAG?
VEEL TE VER-MOEIEND!

Samen sterk

CÉDRIC!
IK WIL NIET DAT JE DE HELE TIJD OP JE SMARTPHONE ZIT TE SPELEN, EN AL HELEMAAL NIET TIJDENS HET ETEN. DAT HEB IK JE AL HONDERD KEER GEZEGD.
PAPA HEEFT GELIJK! IK WORD ER OOK GEK VAN.
ZEG, JE LUISTERT NIET EENS ALS IK TEGEN JE PRAAT. NU HEB IK ER GENOEG VAN. IK NEEM 'M IN BESLAG!
MAAR... HEE, WAT BEZIELT JE? WAT MOET IK ZONDER M'N TELEFOON DOEN? IK HEB HEM NODIG!
IK LEG 'M HIER, MAAR JE RAAKT 'M DE HELE WEEK NIET AAN, BEGREPEN?
EEN HELE WEEK? PFT, VOLGENDE WEEK IS HIJ UIT DE MODE OF BEN IK TE OUD OM 'M NOG TE KUNNEN GEBRUIKEN.
NU OVERDRIJF JE TOCH ECHT, KNUL.
TOEN IK ZO OUD WAS ALS JIJ, BESTONDEN AL DIE MACHIENTJES NIET. VRIENDJES SPEELDEN SAMEN EN SPRAKEN NOG ECHT MET ELKAAR. DAT WAS HEEL WAT GEZELLIGER.
MIJN VRIENDEN ZULLEN ME UITLACHEN. DIT IS VERNEDEREND!
494/1

DE VOLGENDE DAG.
HOI, CÉDRIC. HEE, WAT KIJK JE KWAAD. WAT IS ER?
NIKS!
NIKS? WAAROM KIJK JE DAN ALSOF JE NET VAN 'N BEGRAFENIS KOMT?
ER IS NIKS, ZEG IK JE!
VERTEL! NATUURLIJK IS ER IETS GEBEURD.
HET IS EEN RAMP. M'N VADER HEEFT M'N TELEFOON IN BESLAG GENOMEN. IK KRIJG 'M DE HELE WEEK NIET MEER TERUG.
WAT?
EEN HELE WEEK! HOE MOET IK JE DAN APPEN? DAT KAN TOCH HELEMAAL NIET.
VIND IK OOK.
WAT IS EL MET CÉDLIC?
HIJ IS KWAAD. Z'N VADER HEEFT Z'N TELE-FOON IN BESLAG GENOMEN. HIJ KRIJGT 'M DE HELE WEEK NIET TERUG.
EEN HELE WEEK?! DAT IS VELSCHLIKKELIJK.
ZULLEN WE HET JUFFROUW NELLY VERTELLEN? MISSCHIEN KAN ZIJ HELPEN... ONDERHANDELEN MET Z'N OUDERS.
IK DENK DAT HIJ NAAR EEN PSYCHOLOOG MOET.
JE MOET JE TELEFOON OP EEN OF ANDERE MANIER TERUGKRIJGEN.
IK HEB EEN IDEE.
LUISTER, WE DOEN HET VOLGENDE: ....
494/2

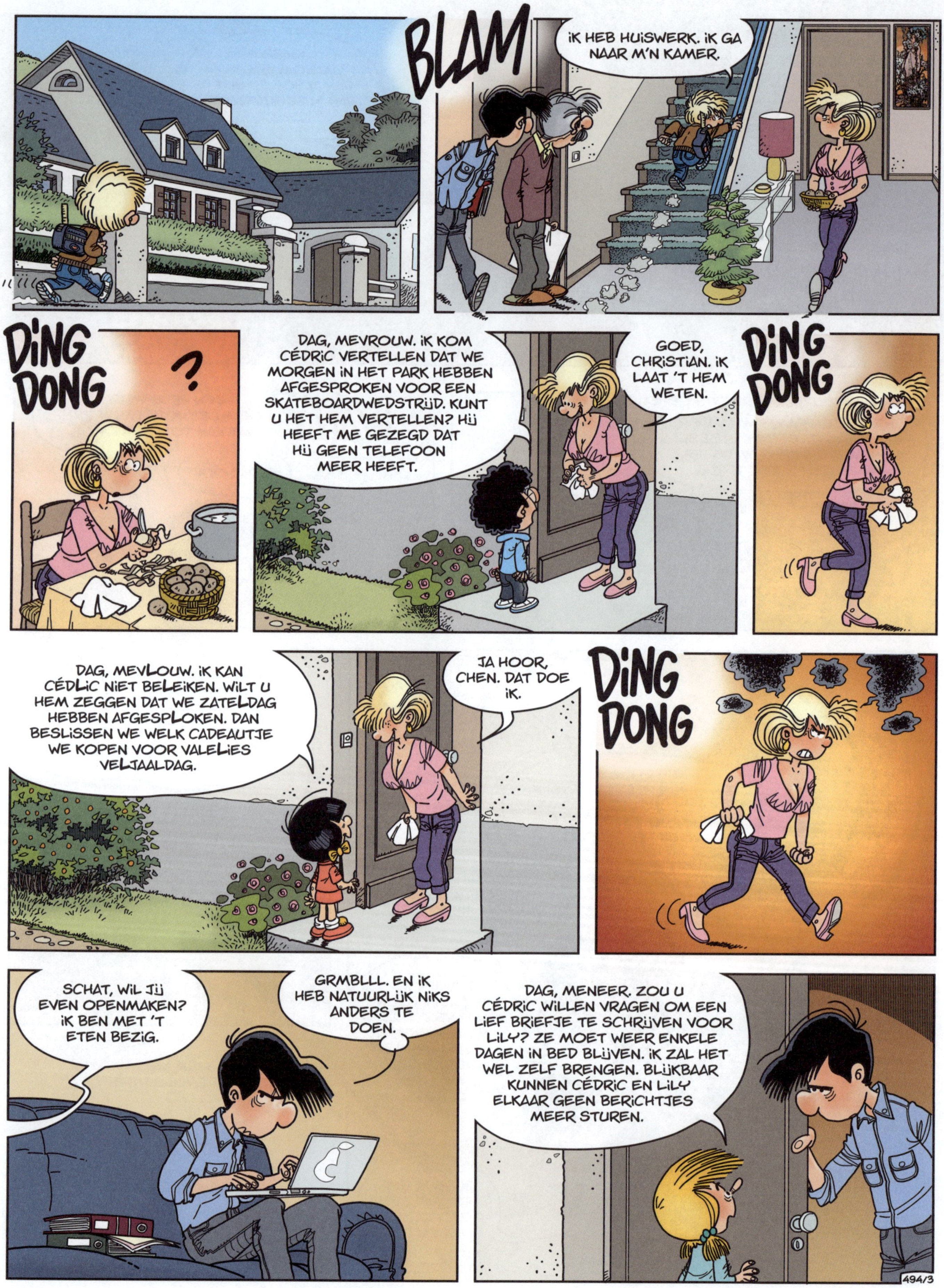
BLAM
IK HEB HUISWERK. IK GA NAAR M'N KAMER.
DING DONG
?
DAG, MEVROUW. IK KOM CÉDRIC VERTELLEN DAT WE MORGEN IN HET PARK HEBBEN AFGESPROKEN VOOR EEN SKATEBOARDWEDSTRIJD. KUNT U HET HEM VERTELLEN? HIJ HEEFT ME GEZEGD DAT HIJ GEEN TELEFOON MEER HEEFT.
GOED, CHRISTIAN. IK LAAT 'T HEM WETEN.
DING DONG
DAG, MEVLOUW. IK KAN CÉDLIC NIET BELEIKEN. WILT U HEM ZEGGEN DAT WE ZATELDAG HEBBEN AFGESPLOKEN. DAN BESLISSEN WE WELK CADEAUTJE WE KOPEN VOOR VALELIES VELJAALDAG.
JA HOOR, CHEN. DAT DOE IK.
DING DONG
SCHAT, WIL JIJ EVEN OPENMAKEN? IK BEN MET 'T ETEN BEZIG.
GRMBLLL. EN IK HEB NATUURLIJK NIKS ANDERS TE DOEN.
DAG, MENEER. ZOU U CÉDRIC WILLEN VRAGEN OM EEN LIEF BRIEFJE TE SCHRIJVEN VOOR LILY? ZE MOET WEER ENKELE DAGEN IN BED BLIJVEN. IK ZAL HET WEL ZELF BRENGEN. BLIJKBAAR KUNNEN CÉDRIC EN LILY ELKAAR GEEN BERICHTJES MEER STUREN.
494/3

JE HEBT TOCH GEEN HALFUUR NODIG OM TWEE ZINNETJES OP PAPIER TE ZETTEN, NEEM IK AAN?
EEN SMS'JE GAAT NATUURLIJK SNELLER.
DANK U, MENEER.
GRAAG GEDAAN!
DING DONG
NEE, HÈ!
WILT U CÉDRIC ZEGGEN DAT WE DE SKATEBOARDWEDSTRIJD VAN MORGEN UITSTELLEN?
AH? OKÉ!
BLAM
PFT! ALS IK NIET VERPLICHT WAS OM THUIS TE WERKEN, ZAT IK NU LEKKER RUSTIG OP DE ZAAK EN KON IK OPSCHIETEN!
DING DONG
DAG, MENEER. IK WOU...
JA, IK ZAL 'T ZEGGEN!
BLAM
CÉDRIC... KOM EVEN HIER!
IK SCHELD JE STRAF KWIJT. HIER IS JE TELEFOON.
NU AL?
494/4
STANDVASTIGHEID IS ANDERS WEL BELANGRIJK IN OPVOEDING.
'T IS AL GOED. HOU MAAR OP!
BLIP TUUUT BLIP TUU BLIP
BLIP BLIP BLIP TUUUT TUUT
TUUU BLIP BLIP

Opa maakt zich druk

Wat 'n dag

TOT STRAKJES, PAPA. IK GA WERKEN.
IK KOM VANMIDDAG HIER ETEN.
HMMM...
CÉDRIC ZIT IN Z'N KAMER. ER IS EEN PEDAGOGISCHE DAG EN DE KINDEREN HEBBEN GEEN SCHOOL.
HEBBEN DIE KINDEREN NU WEER VAKANTIE? ZE ZITTEN MEER THUIS DAN OP SCHOOL.
DAT WAS IN MIJN TIJD WEL ANDERS. WIJ MOESTEN ELKE DAG NAAR SCHOOL.
JUIST. TOT VANMIDDAG.
WAAR IS M'N KRANT? O, DIE HEB IK VAST BOVEN LATEN LIGGEN.
KLAK KLAK KLAK KLAK KLAK
PLOP PLOP PLOP PLOP
498/1

RHA!
M'N BRIL!...
KLAK KLAK KLAK KLAK KLAK
PLOP PLOP PLOP PLOP
TOEN IK M'N BRIL GING HALEN, HAD IK NET ZO GOED M'N BLOEDDRUKPILLEN MEE KUNNEN BRENGEN. HET IS BIJNA TIJD.
KLAK KLAK KLAK KLAK KLAK
PLOP PLOP PLOP PLOP
POLITICS
BILL GATES BIEDT $ 10.000.000 VOOR DE PET VAN TRUMP.
OPA, WIL JE EVEN NAAR M'N KAMER KOMEN?
?
KLAK KLAK KLAK KLAK KLAK
498/2

WIL JIJ ALSJEBLIEFT MIJN ELEKTRISCH KLAVIER VAN DE KAST NEMEN? IK KAN ER NIET BIJ.
MMFFF!... IK KAN ER ZELF OOK NIET AAN.
WIE HAALT HET IN Z'N HOOFD OM DAT DING DAAR TE ZETTEN? WAT NU?
GOED, IK HAAL 'N LADDERTJE UIT DE KELDER. WEET JE ZEKER DAT JE NIET MET WAT ANDERS WILT SPELEN?
NEE, IK WIL M'N PIANO. ANDERS HAD IK 'M NIET GEVRAAGD.
PLOP PLOP PLOP PLOP
PLOP PLOP PLOP PLOP
KLAK KLAK KLAK KLAK KLAK
KLAK KLAK KLAK KLAK KLAK
498/3

ZO, HIER IS JE KLAVIER.
IK HEB GEEN ZIN MEER. IK SPEEL WEL OP M'N IPAD.
PLOP PLOP PLOP PLOP
PLOP PLOP PLOP PLOP
KLAK KLAK KLAK KLAK KLAK
HALLO, IK BEN ER!
PAPA!...
SCHAAM JE! TOEN IK VANOCHTEND VERTROK, ZAT JE NET ZO IN JE FAUTEUIL! HET IS NIET GEZOND VOOR JE OM DE HELE DAG TE BLIJVEN ZITTEN! JE MOET DRINGEND MEER BEWEGEN!
498/4

Een donker gezicht zetten

'n Gezellige avond

WIND JE NIET OP, CÉDRIC. IK VIND HET OOK VERVELEND DAT DE WIFI IS UITGEVALLEN. IK WAS NET M'N KERSTMENU AAN HET SAMEN-STELLEN.
DA'S NIET ZO ERG. WE ZULLEN OP KERSTAVOND WEL IN EEN RESTAURANT GAAN ETEN. MAAR MIJN SPELLETJE... DIT IS EEN RAMP! ALS M'N VRIENDEN MORGEN HOREN DAT IK NOG STEEDS OP NIVEAU ÉÉN ZIT, MAAK IK ME HOPELOOS BELACHELIJK. DIT IS VERNEDEREND!
KLAAG NIET ZO. ZONDER INTERNET-VERBINDING KAN IK DE LAATSTE FACTUREN VAN HET JAAR NIET MAKEN. DAARDOOR LOPEN WE GELD MIS. M'N BAAS ZAL HEEL BOOS ZIJN. MISSCHIEN KRIJG IK NU M'N EINDEJAARS-PREMIE NIET.
ALS JIJ NIET ZO ENTHOUSIAST WAS INGEGAAN OP HET VOORSTEL VAN JE BAAS OM THUIS TE WERKEN, ZAT JE NIET IEDERE AVOND HIER VOOR JE COMPUTER. DAN KON JE DIE REKENINGEN RUSTIG OVERDAG IN DE ZAAK MAKEN.
INDERDAAD. WANT OM JOU NIET TE STOREN, MOET IK NU IEDERE AVOND HET GELUID VAN DE TELEVISIE STILLER ZETTEN, WAARVOOR DANK. IK HOOR AL ZO SLECHT!
WEES BLIJ DAT IK IEDERE AVOND VOOR M'N COMPUTER ZIT. ZO KUNT U TENMINSTE MEE-ETEN. MET DAT PENSIOENTJE VAN U ZOU HET ANDERS VAKER BESCHUIT ZIJN DAN BIEFSTUK.
ALS IK STOOR, ZEG JE 'T MAAR. DAN GA IK WEL NAAR 'N TEHUIS. DAN MOET IK HELEMAAL NIET MEER MEE-ETEN!
PAPA!
WILLEN JULLIE ALLEBEI WAT DIMMEN, ALSJEBLIEFT? IK WEET ZEKER DAT ER OVER ENKELE OGENBLIKKEN WEER INTERNET IS.
507/2

JULLIE ZIJN VERSLAAFD AAN DIE ELEKTRONISCHE PRULLEN. EN DAARDOOR IS HET NIET MEER MOGELIJK OM TE GENIETEN VAN EEN GEZELLIGE AVOND THUIS.
JE OVERDRIJFT, PAPA.
IK OVERDRIJF HELEMAAL NIET. VROEGER ZATEN WE OP WINTERAVONDEN ROND HET VUUR GEZELSCHAPSSPELLETJES TE SPELEN. IEDEREEN WAS TOEN RUSTIG EN OPGEWEKT.
IK HEB TROUWENS EEN IDEE. WACHT MAAR EVEN.
KEN JE DIT NOG, MARIE-ROSE? WE SPEELDEN DIT HEEL VAAK MET GERMAINE.
?
?
?
WAT IS DIT?
AUTOPOLY. EEN GEZELSCHAPSSPEL.
HEB JE ER 'N PASWOORD VOOR NODIG?
AUTOPOLY
KOM, GA AAN TAFEL ZITTEN. DAN LEER IK JULLIE HOE EEN GEZELLIGE AVOND ERUITZIET.
EEN SPELER MAG ZIJN AUTO'S ENKEL PARKEREN IN EEN STRAAT WAARVAN HIJ ALLE KLEURKAARTEN BEZIT. IS DAT DUIDELIJK?
MARIE-ROSE HOUDT DE BANK.
GOED.
WAT 'N STOM SPEL. IK HEB NIET EENS EEN JOYSTICK.
AUTOPOLY
507/3

IK GOOI ZEVEN. IK SPRING DUS ZEVEN VAKJES VOORUIT. EEN, TWEE, DRIE, VIER, VIJF, ZES, ZEVEN.
HEE, U ZEGT ZEVEN, MAAR U SPRINGT ER ACHT VOORUIT.
NEE HOOR. IK GING ER ZEVEN VOORUIT.
IK HEB ZE GETELD, HET WAREN ER ACHT!
O JA!? DAN VERBAAST HET ME NIET DAT JE MATTEN ZO DUUR ZIJN... ALS JE NIET BETER KUNT TELLEN!
LAAT DE MATTEN-VERKOPER U DAN OOK EVEN WAT ZEGGEN. IK...
PAPA!
ROBERT!
HET IS MIJN BEURT OM TE SPELEN. IK KOOP EEN AUTOBUS.
?!
IK KOOP OOK EEN AUTOBUS!
JIJ KUNT HELEMAAL GEEN AUTOBUS KOPEN, WANT JE HEBT MAAR TWEE AUTO'S. DAT IS NIET GENOEG.
EEN MINIBUS DAN?
ER ZIJN GEEN MINIBUSSEN.
IK WIL OOK EEN BUS ZOALS MAMA!
DOMME JONGEN! JE MOET VIER AUTO'S HEBBEN VOOR JE EEN AUTOBUS KUNT KOPEN!
PAPA!
ALS IK GEEN AUTOBUS KRIJG, STOP IK!
LAAT HEM DAN TOCH EEN BUS KOPEN! JE HEBT HET TEGEN EEN KIND, ZEG!
MAAR... VOLGENS DE SPELREGELS KAN HET NIET.
ROBERT!

GEFELICITEERD MET JULLIE OPVOEDING. KNAP GEDAAN!
BLIJF RUSTIG, PAPA. SPEEL NU MAAR!
HOP! VIER EN VIER.
JE GOOIT AL VOOR DE DERDE KEER EEN DUBBEL CIJFER. JE MOET NAAR DE GEVANGENIS.
NAAR DE GEVANGENIS? IK GOOI PAS VOOR DE TWEEDE KEER EEN DUBBEL!
DRIE KEER! JE VERGIST JE!
HAHA, OPA MOET NAAR DE GEVANGENIS. GOED ZO!
CÉDRIC!
MARIE-ROSE VERGIST ZICH ZELDEN! GELOOF HAAR MAAR!
O?! DE DAG WAAROP ZE BESLOOT MET JOU TE TROUWEN, BEGING ZE ANDERS WEL DE VERGISSING VAN HAAR LEVEN!
PAPA!
EEN AUTOBUS!
IK WIL EEN AUTOBUS!
CÉDRIC, ZWIJG OVER DIE AUTOBUS!
U EN DIE GEZELSCHAPSSPELLETJES VAN U ZULLEN ME BIJBLIJVEN TOT MIJN ALLERLAATSTE DAG!
TROUWENS, DIT DOE IK ERMEE!
ROBERT, NEE!
ALS WE ONZE AVONDEN IN DE TOEKOMST ZO SAMEN MOETEN DOORBRENGEN, BLIJF IK HIER GEEN DAG LANGER WONEN!
PAPA!
OPGERUIMD STAAT NETJES!
HOOR JE DAT, MARIE-ROSE? HIJ WIL ME HET HUIS UIT!
ACH NEE!
AUTOPOLY
SPREEK IK MET DE DIENST STORINGEN? KUNNEN JULLIE ERVOOR ZORGEN DAT WE ZO SNEL MOGELIJK WEER EEN INTERNETVERBINDING HEBBEN?
NIET MORGEN! VANDAAG!

IK WIL NIET ..ONGEDULDIG LIJKEN, MAAR WANNEER MAG IK LEZEN ?

CAMBRIDGE
UNIVERSITY PRESS

Cambridge Lower Secondary

Global Perspectives

LEARNER'S SKILLS BOOK 9

Keely Laycock

CAMBRIDGE
UNIVERSITY PRESS

University Printing House, Cambridge CB2 8BS, United Kingdom

One Liberty Plaza, 20th Floor, New York, NY 10006, USA

477 Williamstown Road, Port Melbourne, VIC 3207, Australia

314–321, 3rd Floor, Plot 3, Splendor Forum, Jasola District Centre, New Delhi – 110025, India

79 Anson Road, #06–04/06, Singapore 079906

Cambridge University Press is part of the University of Cambridge.

It furthers the University's mission by disseminating knowledge in the pursuit of education, learning and research at the highest international levels of excellence.

www.cambridge.org
Information on this title: www.cambridge.org/9781108790567

20 19 18 17 16 15 14 13 12 11 10

Printed in Italy by L.E.G.O. S.p.A.

A catalogue record for this publication is available from the British Library

ISBN 978-1-108-79056-7 Paperback

Contents

> Introduction

Global Perspectives is all about helping you to develop a range of important skills that will aid you not only in your school and academic life but also in your future career. For example, in any job it's likely that you'll need to do some research, evaluate the information sources you find and of course you'll need to *communicate* what you have found out to others. Getting a job might seem a long way off now, but even at school, communicating with others is really important. For example, when writing a review of a film or book or taking part in a debate about a global issue. As you get older, you will increasingly be asked to *reflect* on how well an activity or a piece of work has gone. In studying Global Perspectives, you learn how to develop these really important practical skills as you explore fascinating topical issues and learn about different points of view from around the world.

This Learner's Skills Book follows on from Learner's Skills Book 8 and is designed so that you can continue to develop skills in research, analysis, evaluation, reflection, collaboration and communication as well as to understand what is meant by each of these terms. You will be using these skills (all apart from collaboration) to write an individual research report which is the Stage 9 Checkpoint. You will see that there is no dedicated section for the skill of collaboration although there are plenty of activities within the other sections that ask you to collaborate with your peers. Section 6 has been dedicated to taking you through the requirements for the Checkpoint from planning to writing to reviewing your Checkpoint. As in the Learner's Skills Book for Stages 7 and 8, each skills section (apart from Section 6 Checkpoint) follows the same approach, guiding you through a 'Starting with', 'Developing' and 'Getting better at' scaffold, building your awareness of your progress and allowing you to take charge of your own learning journey. Section 6 checkpoint guides you with planning, writing and reviewing your Checkpoint. A range of activities and tasks is included in all sections of this Learner's Skills Book, with plenty of opportunities for peer-to-peer and group work, and to enable you to reflect on your progress, track your achievements and record your next steps.

The learner's skills books for Global Perspectives 7–9 are write-in resources, so you can create and keep a portfolio of your work and track your progression through each skill and each stage as you head towards the Checkpoint assessment at the end of Stage 9. When responding to the Independent reflection activities at the end of each lesson and to the Self-assessment activities to set learning targets, I encourage you to take the time to answer these questions about your own learning as honestly as possible. Being aware of how you learn will help you to learn more effectively, and this will be a very valuable skill for you to have. When planning and writing your Checkpoint in Section 6, you might find it useful to use an online document that you can amend and add to as you work through the sections in the Learner's Skills Book.

I hope that you will continue to enjoy exploring a wide range of global topics and discovering different viewpoints from around the world – these, and the skills you will learn and develop, will equip you in countless ways – in school, in your career and in your life.

Keely Laycock

How to use this book

This book contains lots of different features that will help your learning. These are explained below.

These are the learning objectives that will be covered in each lesson.

1.3 Select most suitable methods and conduct research to test predictions and answer a research question

1.4 Select, organise and effectively record relevant information from a wide range of sources and findings from research, justifying the method chosen

This list sets out what you will learn in each lesson. You can use these learning goals to identify what you are learning in the lesson.

My learning goals are to develop my knowledge and understanding about:

- selecting the most suitable research methods
- writing questions to gain relevant information from the internet
- writing questions to gain relevant information from other people
- referencing sources of information accurately.

This will help you to know when you have met your learning goals.

How will I know if I reach my goals?

As you work through this lesson and you achieve your learning goals, tick the 'Achieved' box to show you have completed this. If you haven't quite achieved your learning goals, tick 'Not there yet'. Start to think about how you are going to show your learning goals in your challenge. Add an example from your challenge once you have achieved each learning goal.

Lesson 6	Not there yet	Achieved	Example
I can write questions to gain relevant information from others.			
I can record the information gained from questions asked.			
I can present relevant information from research in a suitable way.			

These are questions or tasks to help check your level of understanding before beginning a lesson.

Prior learning

1 Discuss and answer this question with your partner.

Why might you need to use primary and secondary sources of information?

a Primary ....

....

b Secondary ....

....

Each tip provides useful information and key points to consider.

Tip

A consequence is a result of something happening.

This focuses on how you are learning, rather than what you are learning, and you can set yourself learning targets for the next lesson/s.

Independent reflection activity

Which part of today's lesson did you find the most difficult?

....

....

Why do you think this was?

....

....

How are you going to get better at this?

....

....

These are check-ins at the end of each lesson, to encourage you to reflect on your progression through the learning goals, and relate this to your Challenge topic.

Check your learning

If you haven't already done so, complete the **How will I know if I reach my goals?** table with 'Not there yet' or 'Achieved'. Don't forget to add examples from your challenge.

This allows you to consider your progress through the learning goals. The red-amber-green checklist encourages you to think about where you are on your learning journey, and to look back at past self-assessments to see clearly how you are progressing.

Self-assessment 3

Look back at self-assessments 1 and 2. How much further progress do you feel you have made so far in developing your evaluation skills?

For each learning objective in the table below, shade in the response that matches yours most closely. Give one example for this response. Eventually, you are aiming for green!

Learning objectives: *to get better at ...*	RED	AMBER	GREEN
3.1 Evaluate a range of sources, considering the author and purpose and how well they are supported by other sources, explaining why some may be biased.	I can explain what evaluation is. I can recognise if information sources contain bias with help. I can identify the audience for and the purpose of different information sources with help.	I can explain what evaluation is. I can recognise if information sources contain bias. I can identify the audience for and the purpose of different information sources.	I can explain what evaluation is. I can recognise if information sources contain bias or are biased. I can explain the audience for and the purpose of different information sources. I can help others recognise bias in information sources and the audience for and purpose of different information sources.

This provides an opportunity to reflect on your Challenge topic as you progress through each skill.

Challenge topic review

Think about the challenge topic you have been exploring and complete the following statements.

I was surprised to discover that ....

....

I didn't know ....

....

I now think ....

....

Register to access free supporting resources through Cambridge GO – the home for all of your Cambridge digital content. Visit cambridge.org/go

Checkpoint features

Checklist

Use these checklists to review your Checkpoint draft against what you've learnt in lessons, and create action points to progress your learning.

Checklist 1

Look at Checklist 1. How much progress have you made?

Review your planning for your draft Checkpoint by completing the table below. For each of the criteria, tick 'YES' or 'NO'. Where you have ticked 'NO', add at least one action point. Eventually, you are aiming for 'YES' for each of the criteria.

CRITERIA *I have…*	Yes	No	ACTION POINT (e.g. Make my global perspective clearer and more explicit; explain causes more fully; add transition words for comparing global and national perspectives)
formulated a focused research question			
explained relevant causes and consequences			
included relevant information from different sources			
presented a clear and explicit global perspective			

Next steps

Reflect on your action points to summarise the next steps you need to take with your Checkpoint.

Next steps

Reflect on your responses to Checklist 1. Summarise what you need to do before you are ready to write the next draft of your Checkpoint research report.

I need to ....

....

....

....

Section 1

Research

This section of your Learner's Skills Book helps you to develop your research skills using interesting global topics.

Starting with . . .

As you start to develop your research skills in Stage 9, you will be learning to discuss the features of effective research, evaluate and write relevant research questions, choosing which research question might be suitable for a research report. You will also learn to select suitable research methods to help answer a research question, select relevant information from a source and summarise this information in your own words. You will explore how to reference information sources accurately and use references to find relevant information.

Developing . . .

As you further develop your research skills in Stage 9, you will be discussing and explaining the features of good research questions, evaluating and rewording research questions and formulating research questions that help write reports including specific features, such as a global and national perspective and a course of action. You will also be developing your understanding about how to select the most suitable research methods depending on your aim and you will write questions to gain information about a topic from both the internet and other people.

Getting better at . . .

As you get better at research during Stage 9, you will be exploring how research helps to test a prediction, which includes conducting research and writing questions to help answer a research question that tests a prediction. You will understand why we use primary and secondary information sources, and get better at evaluating research questions and gaining and recording relevant information from an information source. You will also get better at presenting the information you find to an audience using a suitable method of your choice.

1

Starting with research skills: Lesson 1

1.1 Construct a range of relevant research questions and identify the most appropriate one to follow up

My learning goals are to start to:

- discuss the features of effective research
- evaluate research questions
- write relevant research questions

How will I know if I reach my goals?

As you work through this lesson and you achieve your learning goals, tick the 'Achieved' box to show you have completed this. If you haven't quite achieved your learning goals, tick 'Not there yet'. Start to think about how you are going to show your learning goals in your challenge. Add an example from your challenge once you have achieved each learning goal.

Lesson 1	Not there yet	Achieved	Example
I can discuss the features of effective research.			
I can evaluate a research question.			
I can write a research question.			

Prior learning

1 Which of these features are part of effective research and which are not? Discuss this with a partner.

A Looking at an author's webpage to see where they work, their expertise and what else they have published.

B Copying and pasting relevant information from a newspaper article found on the internet.

C Making notes from an information source to answer questions relevant to a research study.

D Recording the title of an article, the date published and the author's name to add to a reference list.

....

....

2 Do your classmates agree with you? Yes/No

Why? ....

....

3 Add one further feature to explain how to conduct effective research.

....

Tip

Effective research enables you to find relevant information to help answer a research question; it helps you to find facts/statistics and evidence to support your own points; it helps you to check information that you might have got from a different source.

Starter activity

The topic I am working on today is ...

....

1 Look at the research questions your teacher gives you. Discuss them with your partner and answer the following for each question:

a Is the question interesting?

b Is the question clear?

c Is the question too broad, too narrow or too vague?

d Is the question a leading question?

e Can the question be answered after research?

Question 1 ....

Question 2 ....

Question 3 ....

Question 4 ....

Question 5 ....

2 a Look at the research questions again. Which one question do you think is the best research question to allow you to do the following?

a Explain a range of causes and consequences

b Develop a global perspective

c Develop a national perspective

d Propose a course of action

e Reflect on how your personal perspective has changed or developed

Question: ....

Tip

A global perspective is thinking about a situation or issue as it relates to the whole world. For example, 'According to the World Health Organization, children and young people between the ages of 5 and 17 should participate in at least 60 minutes of physical activity per day.' This is global as the World Health Organization is a global organisation.

Tip

A course of action is something you do to try to help resolve an issue. For example, you might hold a cake sale to raise money for a charity that helps people affected by conflict.

> **Tip**
>
> A national perspective is thinking about a situation or issue as it relates to a specific country. For example, 'The National Health Service in the United Kingdom agrees that it is important that children and young people take part in at least 60 minutes of physical activity per day.'

b Do your classmates agree?

Main activity

The topic I am working on today is …

....

1 Consider the topic your teacher has chosen. Discuss it with a partner. Produce a mind map of as many questions about the topic as you can think of.

> **Tip**
>
> A personal perspective is what you think, supported by evidence. Without evidence, it is just your opinion.

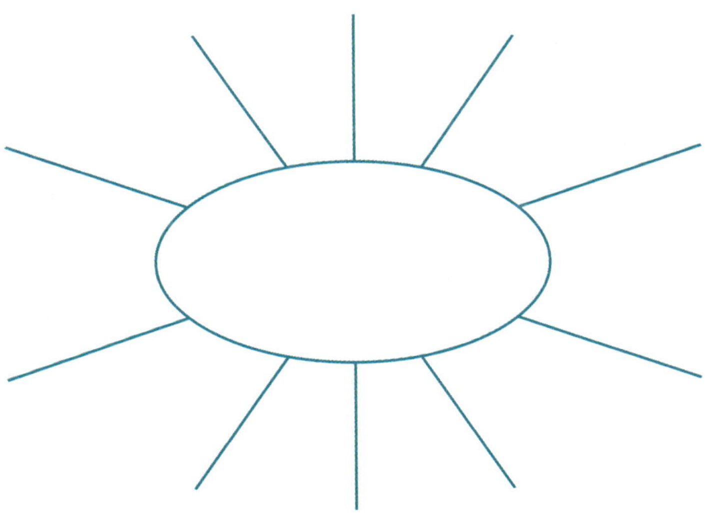

Peer feedback

2 **a** Discuss your questions with another pair to check that they are relevant to the topic.

b Now write down your three best research questions. Remember to check whether each of your questions:

- is interesting
- is clear
- is not leading
- is not too broad, too narrow or too vague
- is arguable
- can be answered after research.

1 ....

....

2 ....

....

3 ....

....

Peer feedback

3 Check your questions with another pair.

4 Now choose one of these three questions. You might need to reword it to make sure your question allows you to:

- explain a range of causes and consequences
- develop a global perspective
- develop a national perspective
- propose a course of action
- draw a conclusion (answer the question and reflect on how your perspective has changed or developed).

Question: ....

....

Class discussion

After class discussion, write down the best research question and explain why you think it is the best.

Best research question is ....

....

Because ....

....

Independent reflection activity

What do you think has helped you develop your research skills in this lesson? Explain why.

- A Discussing the features of effective research
- B Evaluating research questions
- C Writing research questions

....

....

....

Which of these other skills do you think you have used today? Explain how you used them.

- A Communication skills
- B Collaboration skills
- C Reflection skills

....

....

....

Check your learning

If you haven't already done so, complete the **How will I know if I reach my goals?** table with 'Not there yet' or 'Achieved'. Don't forget to add examples from your challenge.

2

Starting with research skills: Lesson 2

1.3 Select most suitable methods and conduct research to test predictions and answer a research question

1.4 Select, organise and effectively record relevant information from a wide range of sources and findings from research, justifying the method chosen

My learning goals are to start to:

- select suitable research methods to help answer a research question
- select relevant information from an information source
- summarise relevant information from an information source

How will I know if I reach my goals?

As you work through this lesson and you achieve your learning goals, tick the 'Achieved' box to show you have completed this. If you haven't quite achieved your learning goals, tick 'Not there yet'. Start to think about how you are going to show your learning goals in your challenge. Add an example from your challenge once you have achieved each learning goal.

Lesson 2	Not there yet	Achieved	Example
I can select suitable research methods to help answer a research question.			
I can select relevant information from an information source.			
I can summarise relevant information from an information source in my own words.			

Prior learning

1 Which of these questions tests a prediction? Discuss with a partner.

A Does eating junk food lead to chronic disease in the UK?

B Why is chronic disease on the increase?

C Are environmental factors responsible for chronic disease?

....

....

2 Do your classmates agree? Yes/No

Why? ....

....

Tip

A prediction is a statement about what you think might happen in the future or what you think might be the cause or consequence of something that has happened.

Starter activity

1 Which of the questions in the Prior learning activity is the best research question to develop a global and national perspective?

....

2 What do you think are the most suitable methods of research for answering the research question identified in task 1?

....

3 What key words (between three and six) would you put into a search engine to help find information to answer the question identified in task 1?

....

Peer feedback

4 Do your classmates agree?

5 Change or add further ideas for tasks 2 and 3 in a different colour.

Main activity

The topic I am working on today is ...

....

1 Discuss the information source your teacher gives you with a partner.

a Formulate a relevant research question that the information source might help you answer.

....

....

Tip

To formulate a research question, you need to reflect on the information source to find out the main ideas.

b Discuss your research question with another pair.
Agree on the best research question.

....

....

2 a Reflect on the source again. In your small group, make notes in the table.

Topic	
Research question	
Feature	**Notes**
Cause(s)	
Consequence(s)	
Global perspective	
National perspective	
Course of action	

Tip

Research is important to find evidence to support a claim or to test a prediction. Without research, what you write is either anecdotal from your own or other people's experience, or opinion lacking evidence to support it.

Peer feedback

b Share your notes. Do your classmates agree that your notes reflect the content of the source? Add further notes if necessary.

3 Choose one of the features from your table in task **2a**. On a separate sheet of paper, write a summary for this feature from your notes.

4 Look at the summaries of the whole group and decide whether they reflect the content of the source but in their own words. Improve them if not.

Tip

To write a summary in your own words, you need to review the source a few times, think about it and then use the notes you have made.

Independent reflection activity

Which part of this lesson have you found the most interesting? Explain why.

A Formulating a research question

B Making notes

C Writing a summary

D Sharing summaries with classmates to get a deeper understanding of an information source

....

....

....

How have you used communication skills in this lesson?

....

....

....

Check your learning

If you haven't already done so, complete the **How will I know if I reach my goals?** table with 'Not there yet' or 'Achieved'. Don't forget to add examples from your challenge.

3

Starting with research skills: Lesson 3

1.2 Identify and accurately reference a wide range of print and multimedia sources and use them to locate relevant information and answer research questions

1.4 Select, organise and effectively record relevant information from a wide range of sources and findings from research, justifying the method chosen

My learning goals are to start to:

- understand how to reference information sources accurately
- use references to find relevant information
- record relevant information

How will I know if I reach my goals?

As you work through this lesson and you achieve your learning goals, tick the 'Achieved' box to show you have completed this. If you haven't quite achieved your learning goals, tick 'Not there yet'. Start to think about how you are going to show your learning goals in your challenge. Add an example from your challenge once you have achieved each learning goal.

Lesson 3	Not there yet	Achieved	Example
I understand how to reference information sources accurately.			
I can use a reference to find relevant information.			
I can record relevant information in a suitable way.			

Prior learning

1 Discuss with a partner. Which of these references is incorrect? Why?

A Khany (2018). 'Known causes of disease.' Online: http://kcd.disease.org/causes/ (accessed 22/07/2019).

B Barnes (2017). 'Diet and lifestyle tips.' Online: http://diet/lifestyle/bl/ (accessed 23/07/2019).

C German Health Agency (2018). 'Ways to prevent chronic disease.' Information leaflet.

D World Health Organization. Online: http://www.health.org/about_our_health/diet/issues/ (accessed 23/07/2019).

E Community (2018). 'How to get healthier.' *Community Newsletter*, March issue.

....

....

2 Do your classmates agree? Yes/No

Why? ....

3 What do you think needs including in a reference for it to be considered accurate?

Why? ....

The topic I am working on today is …

....

Starter activity

1 Look at the information sources your teacher shows you. Discuss them with a partner. Write a reference for each source.

A ....

B ....

C ....

Peer feedback

2 Share your references with your classmates. Did you all agree? Make corrections to your references.

A ....

B ....

C ....

Main activity

1 Look at the references your teacher gives you. Discuss them with a partner. Predict the content of each source.

A ....

B ....

C ....

2 Choose one of the references. Find the source of information using the reference. Discuss the information with a partner. Answer the following questions.

a What is the issue?

....

Tip

A reference list is a list of all the sources of information you have researched and used in your own work.

Tip

When writing a reference, you need to include the title of the article, the date, the author and the name of the publisher. If the source is online, then you also include the website address and the date you accessed the source.

b What causes and/or consequences are mentioned?

....

c What perspectives are referred to?

....

d Are any courses of action given? If so, what are they?

....

e What research question might your source help you answer?

....

Peer feedback

3 Share your answers with another pair who chose the same reference as you. Add any further information to answer the questions in a different colour.

Independent reflection activity

Which part of today's lesson did you find the most challenging? Explain why.

A Writing a reference for a source

B Predicting the content of a source from a reference

C Finding a source of information from a reference

D Identifying information to answer questions about a source

....

....

....

How have you used collaboration skills in today's lesson?

....

....

....

Check your learning

If you haven't already done so, complete the **How will I know if I reach my goals?** table with 'Not there yet' or 'Achieved'. Don't forget to add examples from your challenge.

Self-assessment 1

How much progress do you feel you have made so far in developing your research skills?

For each learning objective in the table below, shade in the response that matches yours most closely. Give one example for this response. Eventually, you are aiming for green!

Learning objectives: *to start to . . .*	RED	AMBER	GREEN
1.1 Construct a range of relevant research questions and identify the most appropriate one to follow up.	I know some of the features of effective research and can evaluate a research question with help.	I know some of the features of effective research. I can evaluate a research question. I can write a research question with help.	I know the features of effective research. I can evaluate a research question. I can help others evaluate research questions. I can write a research question.
1.2 Identify and accurately reference a wide range of print and multimedia sources and use them to locate relevant information and answer research questions.	I understand the importance of referencing. I can reference at least one source accurately. I can find relevant information from a reference with help.	I understand the importance of referencing. I can reference information sources with some accuracy. I can find relevant information from a reference.	I understand the importance of referencing. I can accurately reference information sources. I can find relevant information from a reference and can help others with referencing.
1.3 Select most suitable methods and conduct research to test predictions and answer a research question.	I know what a prediction is and can conduct some research to test a prediction with help.	I know what a prediction is. I can conduct some research to test a prediction.	I know what a prediction is. I can conduct some research to test a prediction and can help others conduct research to test a prediction.

Continued

Learning objectives: *to start to . . .*	RED	AMBER	GREEN
1.4 Select, organise and effectively record relevant information from a wide range of sources and findings from research, justifying the method chosen.	I can select and record some relevant information from an information source with help.	I can select and record some relevant information from an information source.	I can select and record some relevant information from an information source. I can help others select and record some relevant information.

Example:

1.1 ....

1.2 ....

1.3 ....

1.4 ....

Reflect on your responses in your self-assessment and identify two areas for improvement. Set yourself two learning targets – how you will improve upon the two areas. For example: 'I will check that I write down only relevant information from a source and that I write it in my own words.'

Learning targets:

1 Area for improvement: ....

How I will improve: ....

2 Area for improvement: ....

How I will improve: ....

Challenge topic review

Think about the challenge topic you have been exploring and complete the following statements.

I was surprised to discover that ....

....

I didn't know ....

....

I now think ....

....

4

Developing research skills: Lesson 4

1.1 Construct a range of relevant research questions and identify the most appropriate one to follow up

My learning goals are to develop my knowledge and understanding about:

- the features of good research questions
- rewording questions to make them good research questions
- writing relevant research questions to help write reports including specific features

How will I know if I reach my goals?

As you work through this lesson and you achieve your learning goals, tick the 'Achieved' box to show you have completed this. If you haven't quite achieved your learning goals, tick 'Not there yet'. Start to think about how you are going to show your learning goals in your challenge. Add an example from your challenge once you have achieved each learning goal.

Lesson 4	Not there yet	Achieved	Example
I can explain the features of a good research question.			
I can evaluate and reword a research question.			
I can write a relevant research question.			

Prior learning

Discuss the features of a good research question with your partner.
Then finish the following sentence in no more than ten words.

A good research question ....

....

....

Starter activity

1 Which of these is the best research question. Explain why.

- A Why is it important to do sport?
- B Do you agree that football can help bring nations together?
- C Can sport help to reduce crime?

....

....

Peer feedback

2 Do your classmates agree with you?

3 Work with your partner to make the other two questions in task 1 better research questions.

A ....

B ....

C ....

Share with another pair. Do they have similar better research questions?

Main activity

The topic I am working on today is …

....

Choose one of the sub-topics your teacher shows you.
Work through the following tasks.

Chosen sub-topic: ....

....

1 What interests you about the topic?

....

2 Write three research questions to do with the topic.

a ....

....

b ....

....

c ....

....

> **Tip**
>
> A good research question is interesting, clear, can be argued and allows for the development of different perspectives.

3 Look at your questions. Check the following qualities.

a Are they interesting? Yes/No

b Are they clear? Yes/No

c Can they be argued? Yes/No

d Do they allow for the development of different perspectives? Yes/No

4 Reword your questions if necessary.

a ....

....

b ....

....

c ....

....

5 Do some initial research.
Write down one possible research question that allows you to:

- write a clear, interesting, focused report with an answer
- develop a global and national perspective
- propose a national course of action
- give your own personal perspective (after research and exploring a global and national perspective).

Question: ....

....

6 Check your question with your teacher.

7 Reword your question if necessary.

....

....

Tip

A clear research question is a question that someone else can understand and would know what you are asking.

Tip

A focused research question is a question that is not too broad, too narrow or too vague. A question that is too broad makes it hard to find a clear answer. A question that is too narrow makes it hard to find enough information. A question that is too vague makes it difficult to know what to research.

Independent reflection activity

Which part of today's lesson did you find the most interesting. Explain why.

A Discussing the features of a good research question

B Improving research questions

C Writing a research question

D Evaluating a research question

....

....

....

Explain how you have used communication skills in today's lesson.

....

....

....

Check your learning

If you haven't already done so, complete the **How will I know if I reach my goals?** table with 'Not there yet' or 'Achieved'. Don't forget to add examples from your challenge.

5

Developing research skills: Lesson 5

1.1 Construct a range of relevant research questions and identify the most appropriate one to follow up

1.2 Identify and accurately reference a wide range of print and multimedia sources and use them to locate relevant information and answer research questions

1.3 Select most suitable methods and conduct research to test predictions and answer a research question

My learning goals are to develop my knowledge and understanding about:

- selecting the most suitable research methods
- writing questions to gain relevant information from the internet
- writing questions to gain relevant information from other people
- referencing sources of information accurately

How will I know if I reach my goals?

As you work through this lesson and you achieve your learning goals, tick the 'Achieved' box to show you have completed this. If you haven't quite achieved your learning goals, tick 'Not there yet'. Start to think about how you are going to show your learning goals in your challenge. Add an example from your challenge once you have achieved each learning goal.

Lesson 5	Not there yet	Achieved	Example
I can select suitable research methods depending on my aim.			
I can write suitable research questions to gain relevant information from the internet.			
I can write suitable questions to gain relevant information from other people.			
I can reference sources of information accurately.			

Prior learning

1 Look at the picture your teacher shows you.
Discuss it with a partner.
Write down three relevant questions.

a ....

b ....

c ....

2 Discuss your questions with another pair.
Write down one good research question and explain why it is a good one.

....

....

....

Starter activity

1 What do you need to remember when writing questions to gain information from other people? Discuss this with a partner.

1 ....

2 ....

3 ....

Peer feedback

2 Share with another pair. Add two more ideas.

4 ....

5 ....

Main activity

The topic I am working on today is …

....

1 Look back at your research question from the Prior learning activity in this lesson. Now write down as many sub-questions as you can to help you start your research.

> **Tip**
>
> Good questions should not be leading or contain bias. For example: 'Why don't more people do sport to improve their health?' is an example of a biased question and 'Do you agree that junk food is unhealthy?' is an example of a leading question.

Research question	
Sub-questions	
1	
2	
3	
4	
5	
6	
7	
8	
9	
10	

Tip

Good questions should be clearly worded and not give too many options.

Tip

Questions to gain a local or national perspective will focus on asking what people think and why.

2 Which of the sub-questions from task 1 are suitable for internet research and which are suitable to ask other people?

Questions suitable for internet research:	Questions suitable to ask other people:
....	....
....	....
....	....
....	....
....	....
....	....

Tip

You will most probably find the answers to questions to gain relevant information and/or a global perspective by using a search engine on the internet.

Peer feedback

3 Do your classmates agree with your two sets of questions? Make changes if necessary.

4 What do you notice about the two sets of questions?

....

....

5 Find some sources of information on the internet to help you answer the questions in the first column in task 2. Write down the references of these sources.

Question	Reference

Independent reflection activity

What helped you learn today?

....

....

How did you develop your reflection skills in today's lesson?

....

....

....

Check your learning

If you haven't already done so, complete the **How will I know if I reach my goals?** table with 'Not there yet' or 'Achieved'. Don't forget to add examples from your challenge.

6

Developing research skills: Lesson 6

1.3 Select most suitable methods and conduct research to test predictions and answer a research question

1.4 Select, organise and effectively record relevant information from a wide range of sources and findings from research, justifying the method chosen

My learning goals are to develop my knowledge and understanding about:

- writing questions to gain relevant information from others
- recording information gained from questions asked
- presenting relevant information from research in a suitable way

How will I know if I reach my goals?

As you work through this lesson and you achieve your learning goals, tick the 'Achieved' box to show you have completed this. If you haven't quite achieved your learning goals, tick 'Not there yet'. Start to think about how you are going to show your learning goals in your challenge. Add an example from your challenge once you have achieved each learning goal.

Lesson 6	Not there yet	Achieved	Example
I can write questions to gain relevant information from others.			
I can record the information gained from questions asked.			
I can present relevant information from research in a suitable way.			

The topic I am working on today is ...

....

Tip

Asking other people questions is called primary research and primary research enables the researcher to gain a first-hand account of events or opinions about issues.

Prior learning

1 Write down questions to ask other people to find out about the topic your teacher gives you.

1 ....

2 ....

3 ....

4 ....

5 ....

2 Do your classmates have any better questions? If so, write them here.

....

....

Starter activity

Ask five of your classmates your questions from the Prior learning activity. Record their answers.

Question	Answers
1	
2	
3	
4	

Tip

Secondary research comes from secondary sources of information, such as the internet or books. These sources of information are created after a specific event by someone who did not experience it first-hand or is reporting someone else's viewpoint or opinion.

Question	Answers
5	

Main activity

1 Present your research findings from the answers you received in the Starter activity. Make sure you choose the most suitable method of presentation for your findings and your purpose.

Peer feedback

2 Give feedback to your classmates on their research findings. Ask the following questions.

a Is the method of presentation suitable for the aim? Yes/No

b Is the method of presentation suitable for the type of research conducted? Yes/No

c Are all the research findings included within the presentation? Yes/No

d Are the research findings presented in a way that is easy to understand? Yes/No

3 Make any changes to your own research presentation according to the feedback you have received.

4 What other questions might you have asked to be able to present more detailed research findings?

....

....

....

Independent reflection activity

What did you find challenging about today's lesson?

How did you overcome this challenge?

Give two examples of skills you have used today.

1 ....

....

2 ....

....

Check your learning

If you haven't already done so, complete the **How will I know if I reach my goals?** table with 'Not there yet' or 'Achieved'. Don't forget to add examples from your challenge.

Self-assessment 2

Look back at self-assessment 1. How much further progress do you feel you have made so far in developing your research skills?

For each learning objective in the table below, shade in the response that matches yours most closely. Give one example for this response. Eventually, you are aiming for green!

Learning objectives: *to develop knowledge and understanding about how to . . .*	RED	AMBER	GREEN
1.1 Construct a range of relevant research questions and identify the most appropriate one to follow up.	I know the features of effective research. I can write a relevant research question with help.	I know the features of effective research. I can evaluate and write a relevant research question.	I know the features of effective research. I can evaluate and write relevant research questions and can help others write relevant research questions.

Continued

Learning objectives: *to develop knowledge and understanding about how to . . .*	RED	AMBER	GREEN
1.2 Identify and accurately reference a wide range of print and multimedia sources and use them to locate relevant information and answer research questions.	I understand the importance of referencing and can reference at least one source of information with some accuracy and with help.	I understand the importance of referencing. I can reference sources of information with some accuracy.	I understand the importance of referencing. I can reference sources of information with accuracy and can help others with referencing.
1.3 Select most suitable methods and conduct research to test predictions and answer a research question.	I can select suitable research methods with help. I can conduct some research to help answer a research question.	I can select suitable research methods. I can conduct some research to help answer a research question.	I can select suitable research methods. I can conduct some research to help answer a research question and help others conduct relevant research.
1.4 Select, organise and effectively record relevant information from a wide range of sources and findings from research, justifying the method chosen.	I can select and organise some relevant information. I can record some relevant information from an information source in my own words with help.	I can select and organise some relevant information. I can record some relevant information from an information source in my own words.	I can select and organise some relevant information. I can record some relevant information from an information source in my own words. I can help others to select, organise and record relevant information.

Example:

1.1 ....

1.2 ....

1.3 ....

1.4 ....

Continued

Learning objectives: *to develop knowledge and understanding about how to . . .*	RED	AMBER	GREEN

Reflect on your responses in your self-assessment and identify two areas for improvement. Set yourself two learning targets – how you will improve upon the two areas. For example, 'I will help someone in class organise their notes to write a summary of their research findings.'

Learning targets:

1 Area for improvement: ....

How I will improve: ....

2 Area for improvement: ....

How I will improve: ....

Challenge topic review

Think about the challenge topic you have been exploring and complete the following statements.

I was surprised to discover that ....

....

I didn't know ....

....

I now think ....

....

7 Getting better at research skills: Lesson 7

1.1 Construct a range of relevant research questions and identify the most appropriate one to follow up

1.3 Select most suitable methods and conduct research to test predictions and answer a research question

1.4 Select, organise and effectively record relevant information from a wide range of sources and findings from research, justifying the method chosen

My learning goals are to get better at:

- understanding how research helps test a prediction
- conducting research to help test a prediction
- writing questions to gain relevant information to help test a prediction

How will I know if I reach my goals?

As you work through this lesson and you achieve your learning goals, tick the 'Achieved' box to show you have completed this. If you haven't quite achieved your learning goals, tick 'Not there yet'. Start to think about how you are going to show your learning goals in your challenge. Add an example from your challenge once you have achieved each learning goal.

Lesson 7	Not there yet	Achieved	Example
I understand how research helps test a prediction.			
I can conduct research to help test a prediction.			
I can write questions to gain relevant information to help test a prediction.			

Prior learning

1 Discuss what a prediction is with your partner. Explain what a prediction is.

A prediction is ....

....

2 How does research help you to test a prediction? ....

....

Share your ideas in class.

3 Write a research question to test a prediction.

....

....

4 Check your question with your classmates.
Do they agree that your research question helps test a prediction?

....

....

Starter activity

1 Read the source of information your teacher gives you. Discuss it with your partner and then answer the following questions.

a What kind of information source is it?

....

b Why do you think the source was created?

....

c Who created the source?

....

d Who do you think the audience for the source is?

....

e Do you think the source helps test a prediction? Yes/No

Why?...

Class discussion

2 Using your learning from class discussion and a different colour pen, add to or change any of your answers for task 1 (a–e).

Main activity

The topic I am working on today is …

....

1 Choose one of the topics your teacher shows you. Discuss it with a partner. Write a research question that tests a prediction about your chosen topic.

....

....

2 Do your classmates agree that your research question helps test a prediction? Yes/No

If not, change your question and check with your classmates again.

....

....

3 Find a suitable information source that helps to test your prediction. Write five questions about the content of the source for someone else to answer.

Information source: ....

1 ....

2 ....

3 ....

4 ....

5 ....

4 Write the answers to your questions but keep them hidden until someone has answered your questions.

1 ....

2 ....

3 ....

4 ....

5 ....

5 Give your information source and five questions to someone else to answer. Then check their answers.

Independent reflection activity

What has helped you learn today?

....

....

....

....

How have you helped someone else learn today?

....

....

....

....

Check your learning

If you haven't already done so, complete the **How will I know if I reach my goals?** table with 'Not there yet' or 'Achieved'. Don't forget to add examples from your challenge.

8

Getting better at research skills: Lesson 8

1.1 Construct a range of relevant research questions and identify the most appropriate one to follow up

1.3 Select most suitable methods and conduct research to test predictions and answer a research question

1.4 Select, organise and effectively record relevant information from a wide range of sources and findings from research, justifying the method chosen

My learning goals are to get better at:

- understanding why primary and secondary information sources are used
- evaluating research questions
- gaining and recording relevant information from a source

How will I know if I reach my goals?

As you work through this lesson and you achieve your learning goals, tick the 'Achieved' box to show you have completed this. If you haven't quite achieved your learning goals, tick 'Not there yet'. Start to think about how you are going to show your learning goals in your challenge. Add an example from your challenge once you have achieved each learning goal.

Lesson 8	Not there yet	Achieved	Example
I understand why primary and secondary sources of information are used.			
I can evaluate a research question.			
I can gain and record relevant information from a source.			

Prior learning

1 Discuss and answer this question with your partner.

Why might you need to use primary and secondary sources of information?

a Primary ....

....

b Secondary ....

....

2 Give examples of both sources of information.

a Primary ....

b Secondary ....

3 Discuss your answers as a class. Add any further thoughts in a different colour.

The topic I am working on today is …

....

Starter activity

1 Look at the research questions your teacher shows you. Discuss them with a partner. Which is the best research question and why?

Best research question: ....

....

Reason: ....

2 Can you think of a better question?

....

Main activity

1 Using your research question from the Main activity in Lesson 7, find another information source to test your prediction. Discuss the source with a partner. Answer the following questions.

a What kind of information source is it?

....

b Why do you think the source was created?

....

c Who created the source?

....

d Who do you think the audience for the source is?

....

e Do you think the source is reliable? Yes/No

Why? ....

f Do you think the source helps test your prediction? Yes/No

Why? ....

Tip

If the name of a website ends with '.gov' and then a country abbreviation (e.g. '.uk' or '.my'), it is probably a reliable government website.

Tip

If the website ends in '.org', it is probably the website of a non-profit organisation. These websites are good information sources but are probably biased.

Tip

A reliable source is one that lacks bias, is kept updated, is complete and error free, and the author(s) and publication can be checked.

2 Summarise the content of the source in your own words.

a Issue: ....

....

b Cause/consequences: ....

....

c Perspective(s): ....

....

d Course(s) of action: ....

....

3 Write the reference for the source.

....

Tip

If the website address has 'wiki' in it, be careful, as wiki and social media websites can be edited by anyone so the information might not be true. Always cross-reference information obtained from this type of website.

Independent reflection activity

What have you found challenging today?

....

....

How have you addressed this challenge?

....

....

How you have used communication skills today?

....

....

Check your learning

If you haven't already done so, complete the **How will I know if I reach my goals?** table with 'Not there yet' or 'Achieved'. Don't forget to add examples from your challenge.

9

Getting better at research skills: Lesson 9

1.2 Identify and accurately reference a wide range of print and multimedia sources and use them to locate relevant information and answer research questions

1.3 Select most suitable methods and conduct research to test predictions and answer a research question

1.4 Select, organise and effectively record relevant information from a wide range of sources and findings from research, justifying the method chosen

My learning goals are to get better at:

- referencing sources of information
- conducting research to find and record relevant information to answer a research question
- presenting relevant information
- justifying presentation methods

How will I know if I reach my goals?

As you work through this lesson and you achieve your learning goals, tick the 'Achieved' box to show you have completed this. If you haven't quite achieved your learning goals, tick 'Not there yet'. Start to think about how you are going to show your learning goals in your challenge. Add an example from your challenge once you have achieved each learning goal.

Lesson 9	Not there yet	Achieved	Example
I can reference some sources of information accurately.			
I can conduct research to find and record relevant information to help answer a research question.			
I can present relevant information.			
I can explain why I have chosen specific presentation methods.			

Prior learning

Why is it important to do research? Discuss this with a partner.

It is important to do research because ....

....

....

....

The topic I am working on today is …

....

Starter activity

Look at the information you have to answer your research question from the Main activity in Lesson 7. Discuss it with a partner. Answer the following questions:

- a Is all the information relevant to your research question? Yes/No
- b Does your information allow you to explain the causes and/ or consequences of an issue? Yes/No
- c Does the information allow you to develop a global and a national perspective on the issue? Yes/No
- d Does the information allow you to contrast and/or compare the global and national perspective? Yes/No
- e Can you propose a realistic national/local course of action to help resolve your issue? Yes/No
- f Can you include your personal perspective in answering your question? Yes/No
- g Do you need to do further research to present your findings to an audience? Yes/No

Tip

To contrast the national and global perspective, you need to say how the perspectives are similar or different.

Main activity

1 What presentation method have you decided on and why?

Method: ....

Reason: ....

2 What prediction are you testing?

....

....

....

3 What information do you need to include?

....

....

....

....

Tip

Your research question should contain the prediction that you want to test.

Tip

Relevant information includes anything that allows you to draw a conclusion and answer your research question.

4 Create your presentation using your chosen method.

5 Gain feedback on your presentation.
Answer the following questions.

- a Is the research question clear? Yes/No
- b Does the research question test a prediction? Yes/No
- c Are there causes and/or consequences of the issue? Yes/No
- d Has a global perspective been developed? Yes/No
- e Has a national perspective been developed? Yes/No
- f Is there a comparison between the national and global perspective? Yes/No
- g Has a realistic national course of action been presented? Yes/No
- h Is there a conclusion to answer the question, including a personal perspective? Yes/No
- i Have information sources been referenced? Yes/No
- j What improvements are needed?
  1 ....
  2 ....
  3 ....

Tip

Your research question should allow you to explore the causes and consequences of an issue, develop a global and national perspective, and propose a realistic national course of action.

Tip

A realistic course of action is something you can do that will help to resolve an issue.

Independent reflection activity

What skill(s) have you learnt or improved during this lesson?

....

....

What else do you need to do to further develop this/these skill(s)?

....

....

....

Check your learning

If you haven't already done so, complete the **How will I know if I reach my goals?** table with 'Not there yet' or 'Achieved'. Don't forget to add examples from your challenge.

Self-assessment 3

Look back at self-assessments 1 and 2. How much further progress do you feel you have made so far in developing your research skills?

For each learning objective in the table below, shade in the response that matches yours most closely. Give one example for this response. Eventually, you are aiming for green!

Learning objectives: *to get better at understanding how to . . .*	RED	AMBER	GREEN
1.1 Construct a range of relevant research questions and identify the most appropriate one to follow up.	I know some of the features of effective research. I can evaluate a research question with help. I can write a research question with help. I can identify the most appropriate research question to follow up with help.	I know the features of effective research. I can evaluate a research question. I can write a research question. I can identify the most appropriate research question to follow up.	I know the features of effective research. I can evaluate research questions. I can write research questions. I can identify the most appropriate research question to follow up. I can help others evaluate, write and identify suitable research questions to follow up.
1.2 Identify and accurately reference a wide range of print and multimedia sources and use them to locate relevant information and answer research questions.	I understand the importance of referencing. I can reference a source of information accurately with help. I can locate some relevant information from a reference with help.	I understand the importance of referencing. I can reference a source of information accurately. I can locate some relevant information from a reference.	I can select suitable research methods. I know what a prediction is. I understand how to test a prediction using research. I can do an internet search to find some relevant information and can show others how to do research to answer a research question.

Continued

Learning objectives: *to get better at understanding how to . . .*	RED	AMBER	GREEN
1.3 Select most suitable methods and conduct research to test predictions and answer a research question.	I can select suitable research methods with help. I know what a prediction is and have some understanding of how research can help test a prediction. I can do an internet search to find some relevant information to help answer a research question with help.	I can select suitable research methods. I know what a prediction is. I understand how research can help test a prediction. I can do an internet search to find relevant information to help answer a research question.	I can select suitable research methods. I know what a prediction is. I understand how to test a prediction using research. I can do an internet search to find some relevant information and can show others how to do research to answer a research question.
1.4 Select, organise and effectively record relevant information from a wide range of sources and findings from research, justifying the method chosen.	I can select relevant information with help. I can record some relevant information from an information source in my own words. I can present relevant information with help.	I can select relevant information to help answer a research question. I can record relevant information from an information source in my own words. I can present relevant information from an information source and say why I have chosen a particular presentation method.	I can select relevant information to help answer a research question. I can record relevant information from different information sources in my own words and can help others record relevant information in their own words. I can present relevant information from different information sources and explain why I have chosen certain presentation methods.

Continued

Example:

1.1 ....

1.2 ....

1.3 ....

1.4 ....

Reflect on your responses in your self-assessment and identify two areas for improvement. Set yourself two learning targets – how you will improve upon the two areas. For example 'I will help my partner understand how to present their research findings.'

Learning targets:

1 Area for improvement: ....

How I will improve: ....

2 Area for improvement: ....

How I will improve: ....

Challenge topic review

Think about the challenge topic you have been exploring and complete the following statements.

I was surprised to discover that ....

....

I didn't know ....

....

I now think ....

....

Section 2

Analysis

This section of your Learner's Skills Book 9 helps you to develop your analysis skills using interesting global topics.

Starting with . . .

As you start to develop your analysis skills in Stage 9, you will be learning how to explain to someone else what analysis in Global Perspectives is, giving examples to support your explanation. You will analyse ideas and evidence from different sources of information, discussing the issues, perspectives and arguments to show understanding of the sources. You will also start to make links between the causes and consequences of an issue at personal, local and global levels.

Developing . . .

As you further develop your analysis skills in Stage 9, you will discuss actions that can help make a positive difference to or help resolve an issue. You will also explore the possible consequences of taking action to help resolve a national or global issue. You will be given opportunities to identify the patterns and trends in graphs and examine how numerical data can help support an argument. As well as looking at the causes and consequences of issues, you will be able to make connections between these causes and consequences at different levels: global, national and personal.

Getting better at . . .

As you get better at analysing topics and issues in Stage 9, you will be focusing on understanding Global Perspectives key terms, explaining the perspectives of different groups of stakeholders and synthesising arguments and evidence from different information sources. You will use the information gained from research to present your arguments and supporting evidence for a specific perspective on an issue. You will also give and receive feedback to improve a written outcome about an issue from a certain perspective and suggest realistic courses of action to help resolve or make a positive difference to an issue.

Starting with analysis skills: Lesson 1

2.1 Identify perspectives and synthesise arguments and evidence from a range of sources on a given topic

2.3 Make some links between causes and consequences of an issue at personal, local and global levels

My learning goals are to start to:

- explain what analysis means in Global Perspectives, giving supporting examples
- develop a global perspective about an issue
- explain the causes and consequences of an issue at a personal, local or global level

How will I know if I reach my goals?

As you work through this lesson and you achieve your learning goals, tick the 'Achieved' box to show you have completed this. If you haven't quite achieved your learning goals, tick 'Not there yet'. Start to think about how you are going to show your learning goals in your challenge. Add an example from your challenge once you have achieved each learning goal.

Lesson 1	Not there yet	Achieved	Example
I can explain what analysis means in Global Perspectives, giving supporting examples.			
I can develop a global perspective about an issue.			
I can explain the causes and consequences of an issue at a personal, local or global level.			

Prior learning

1 Discuss with a partner. How would you explain to someone else what the term 'analysis' means in Global Perspectives?

....

....

2 Give **two** examples to support your explanation in task 2.

a ....

b ....

3 Share your ideas with another pair. Make any additions or changes to your responses for tasks 1 and 2 in a different colour.

The topic I am working on today is …

....

Starter activity

1 Look at the picture your teacher shows you. Discuss it with a partner. Write down as many words and phrases as you can about the picture in the time your teacher gives you.

....

....

....

....

Peer feedback

2 Discuss the picture and your words and phrases with another pair. Add further words and phrases to your list.

Main activity

1 Choose an issue associated with the picture in the Starter activity. Discuss it with your group.
As a group, answer the following questions.

a What is the issue?

....

....

b What do you think a global perspective about the issue might be? Why?

....

....

Tip

A reason/cause is why something happens.

Tip

A consequence is a result of something happening.

Tip

When discussing the reasons/causes and consequences of something at a personal level, consider the question 'What does it mean to me?'

Tip

When discussing the reasons/causes and consequences of something at a local level, consider the question 'What does it mean to my community?'

c What do you think are the causes/reasons for the issue at a personal, local and global level?

Personal ....

....

Local ....

....

Global ....

....

d What do you think are the consequences of the issue at a personal, local and global level?

Personal ....

....

Local ....

....

Global ....

2 In pairs, do some research to add to your responses for tasks **1c** and **1d** in a different colour.

3 Share your ideas and findings with your group.

Tips

A global perspective is a view on an issue that either has global influence or takes account of the nature of the issue globally.

Analysis can focus on perspectives, viewpoints or reactions to a situation or issue; for example, by giving a detailed explanation about what someone thinks about something and why.

Tip

Analysis is a detailed examination of something, breaking it down into different parts; for example, analysing a text to discover the perspective(s) the ideas come from, the issues within the text and the reasons the text was written.

Tip

Analysis can focus on the causes of or reasons for a situation or issue. It can also focus on the consequences of a situation or issue; for example, losing muscle mass can be a consequence of not exercising enough.

Independent reflection activity

Which part of today's lesson did you find the most challenging?

....

....

Why do you think this was?

....

....

What are you going to do to address this challenge next lesson?

....

....

Check your learning

If you haven't already done so, complete the **How will I know if I reach my goals?** table with 'Not there yet' or 'Achieved'. Don't forget to add examples from your challenge.

2

Starting with analysis skills: Lesson 2

2.2 Identify patterns and trends in graphical or numerical data in order to support an argument

2.3 Make some links between causes and consequences of an issue at personal, local and global levels

My learning goals are to start to:

- recognise links between causes and consequences of an issue at a personal, local or global level
- synthesise information to create a commentary about an issue
- give and receive feedback to improve a commentary about an issue

How will I know if I reach my goals?

As you work through this lesson, tick the 'Achieved' box to show you have achieved your learning goals. If you haven't quite achieved your learning goals, tick 'Not there yet'. Start to think about how you are going to show your learning goals in your challenge. Add an example from your challenge once you have achieved each learning goal.

Lesson 2	Not there yet	Achieved	Example
I can recognise some links between a cause and a consequence at a personal, local or global level.			
I can synthesise information to create a commentary about an issue.			
I can give feedback to improve a commentary about an issue.			

Prior learning

1 In your group, review your notes from the Main activity in Lesson 1. Add any further ideas.

2 What did you learn from class discussion about causes and consequences?

....

....

....

The topic I am working on today is …

....

Tip

A perspective is a certain world view or way of looking at an issue.

Starter activity

1 As a group, list as many words and phrases as you can that will help you write a commentary for your issue. Think of transition words such as 'therefore' and words/phrases that signal causes and consequences.

a Transition words:

....

....

b Words that signal causes:

....

....

c Words that signal consequences:

....

....

2 Share your words/phrases with another group and add more to your list.

> **Tip**
>
> A personal perspective is the view that a person has on an issue after exploring different perspectives and reflecting on the causes and consequences of an issue.

Main activity

1 Work in your group. As a result of the research you started in Lesson 1, write a commentary for your issue, including the information you discovered. Write on a separate sheet of paper. Then record your commentary.

2 Give feedback to another group about their commentary. Answer the following questions.

a Is the issue clear? Yes/No

b Does the commentary include a global perspective on the issue? Yes/No

c Does the commentary include reasons/causes and consequences of the issue? Yes/No

d Does the commentary follow a logical structure? Yes/No

e Give one highlight of the commentary

....

f Give one area for improvement of the commentary

....

> **Tip**
>
> A national perspective is the view that a particular country has on an issue. This is usually explained by the laws, policies and/or speeches made by politicians of that country and might be supported by other groups within that country.

3 Reflecting on what you have learnt, what do you now feel more confident about doing? Why?

....

....

Tip

A learner might develop a global perspective on an issue by examining the causes and/or consequences of the issue across the world and developing a perspective on the issue that takes account of these causes/consequences.

Tip

To synthesise means to bring together ideas from different sources to present an argument or develop a perspective.

Tip

A global perspective is a view on an issue that either has global influence or takes account of the nature of the issue globally. Examples could come from the United Nations, as it is an international agency with global influence.

Independent reflection activity

Which part of this lesson did you find interesting? Why?

....

....

How have you used communication skills today?

....

....

Check your learning

If you haven't already done so, complete the **How will I know if I reach my goals?** table with 'Not there yet' or 'Achieved'. Don't forget to add examples from your challenge.

3

Starting with analysis skills: Lesson 3

2.2 Identify patterns and trends in graphical or numerical data in order to support an argument

2.4 Recommend an appropriate course of action and explain possible consequences for a national or global issue

My learning goals are to start to:

- explain how data from a graph can support an argument
- suggest an appropriate course of action to make a positive difference to an issue
- explain a possible consequence of a course of action

How will I know if I reach my goals?

As you work through this lesson, tick the 'Achieved' box to show you have achieved your learning goals. If you haven't quite achieved your learning goals, tick 'Not there yet'. Start to think about how you are going to show your learning goals in your challenge. Add an example from your challenge once you have achieved each learning goal.

Lesson 3	Not there yet	Achieved	Example
I can explain how data from a graph can support an argument.			
I can suggest an appropriate course of action to make a positive difference to an issue.			
I can explain a possible consequence of a course of action.			

Prior learning

1 Use your prior knowledge and any new learning about reasons/causes, consequences and perspectives to explain the following to your partner:

a A reason/cause is ....

b A consequence is ....

c A perspective is ....

2 Discuss your explanations with a partner. Give an example for each of the following:

a A reason/cause is ....

b A consequence is ....

c A perspective is ....

The topic I am working on today is …

....

Starter activity

1 Look at the graph your teacher shows you. Discuss it with a partner.

2 Write down and answer the questions your teacher gives you.

a ....

....

b ....

....

c ....

....

d ....

....

e ....

....

f ....

....

3 What argument do you think the information gained from this graph might help support?

....

Main activity

1 Look at the data your teacher gives you. Discuss it with your partner. Make some predictions based on the data.

a We predict ....

....

b We predict ....

....

c We predict ....

....

2 Create a double-bar graph using the data. Write a short summary explaining the data to go with your bar graph.

Summary ....

....

Tip

A bar graph can help you present your research findings, but you should also add some text to explain what your bar graph shows.

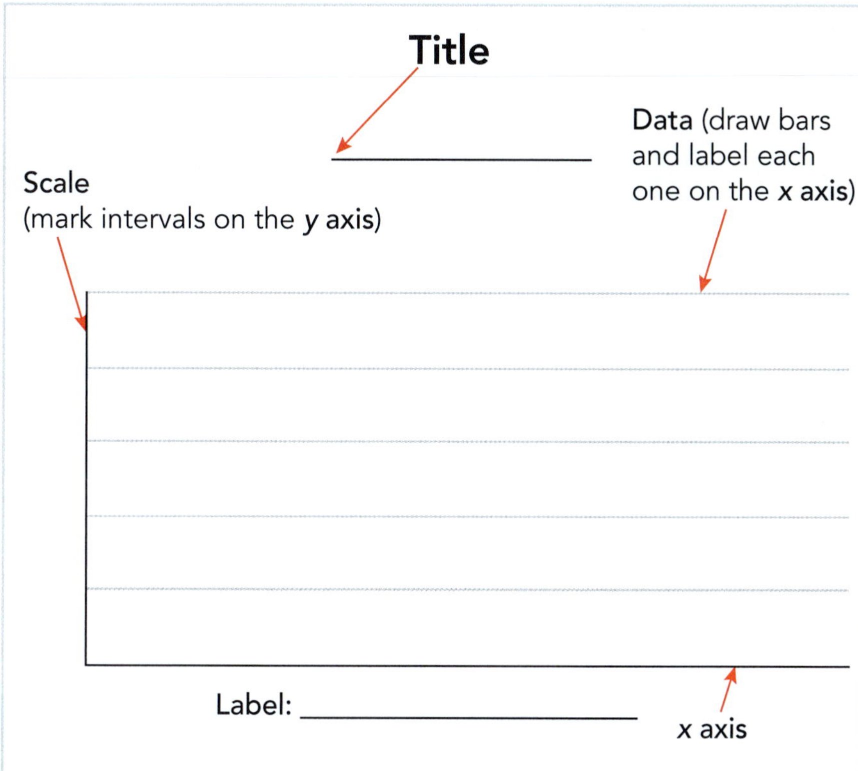

> **Tip**
>
> You can use a bar graph as evidence to support a particular argument you make; for example, the graph shows that young people would do more sport if it were cheaper.

3 Check your predictions from task 1 against your graph. Then answer the following questions.

a How does the data compare with your predictions?

....

b Which of your predictions were close to the actual data?

....

c Which of your predictions were not close to the actual data?

....

> **Tip**
>
> A double-bar graph allows for comparison; for example, between male and female, or between two different countries.

4 Discuss your graph with your classmates. Do the graphs look similar? If not, discuss where the differences are and why there might be differences.

....

5 What course(s) of action might you now take as a result of analysing the data given for tasks 1–4?

....

> **Tip**
>
> A course of action is something you can do to help make a positive difference to an issue.

6 What might be the consequence(s) of the action taken in task 5?

....

Independent reflection activity

What has helped you to learn today?

....

....

How have you helped someone else learn today?

....

....

Check your learning

If you haven't already done so, complete the **How will I know if I reach my goals?** table with 'Not there yet' or 'Achieved'. Don't forget to add examples from your challenge.

Self-assessment 1

How much progress do you feel you have made so far in developing your analysis skills?

For each learning objective in the table below, shade in the response that matches yours most closely. Give one example for this response. Eventually, you are aiming for green!

Learning objectives: *to start to …*	RED	AMBER	GREEN
2.1 Identify perspectives and synthesise arguments and evidence from a range of sources on a given topic.	I can identify at least one perspective with help. I can summarise relevant information from different sources in my own words with help.	I can identify different perspectives with help. I can summarise relevant information from different sources in my own words.	I can identify different perspectives and develop at least one perspective. I can summarise relevant information from different sources in my own words and help others with their summaries.

Continued

Learning objectives: *to start to …*	RED	AMBER	GREEN
2.2 Identify patterns and trends in graphical or numerical data in order to support an argument.	I can identify information from a graph with help. I can create a graph with help. I can say how numerical data can help to support an argument with help.	I can identify information from a graph. I can create a graph. I can say how numerical data can help to support an argument.	I can identify information from a graph and help others identify relevant information. I can create a graph. I can say how numerical data can help to support an argument and help others understand the importance of numerical data.
2.3 Make some links between causes and consequences of an issue at personal, local and global levels.	I can explain what analysis means in Global Perspectives and give some supporting examples with help. I can explain the causes or consequences of an issue at different levels (personal, local, global) with help.	I can explain what analysis means in Global Perspectives and give some supporting examples. I can explain the causes and consequences of an issue at different levels (personal, local, global).	I can explain what analysis means in Global Perspectives and give some supporting examples. I can explain the causes and consequences of an issue at different levels (personal, local, global) and help others explain these.
2.4 Recommend an appropriate course of action and explain possible consequences for a national or global issue.	I can suggest an action to make a positive difference to an issue with help. I can explain the consequences of an action with help.	I can suggest an appropriate course of action to make a positive difference to an issue. I can explain the consequences of an action.	I can suggest an appropriate course of action to make a positive difference to an issue and help others suggest appropriate courses of action for an issue. I can explain the consequences of an action.

Continued

Examples:

2.1 ....

2.2 ....

2.3 ....

2.4 ....

Reflect on your responses in your self-assessment and identify two areas for improvement. Set yourself two learning targets – how you will improve upon the two areas. For example, 'I will ask for some more examples of consequences at a personal level.'

Learning targets:

1 Area for improvement: ....

How I will improve: ....

2 Area for improvement: ....

How I will improve: ....

Challenge topic review

Think about the challenge topic you have been exploring and complete the following statements.

I was surprised to discover that ....

....

I didn't know ....

....

I now think ....

....

4

Developing analysis skills: Lesson 4

2.4 Recommend an appropriate course of action and explain possible consequences for a national or global issue

My learning goals are to develop my knowledge and understanding about:

- appropriate courses of action to help resolve an issue
- possible consequences of taking action to help resolve a national or global issue

How will I know if I reach my goals?

As you work through this lesson, tick the 'Achieved' box to show you have achieved your learning goals. If you haven't quite achieved your learning goals, tick 'Not there yet'. Start to think about how you are going to show your learning goals in your challenge. Add an example from your challenge once you have achieved each learning goal.

Lesson 4	Not there yet	Achieved	Example
I can recommend an appropriate course of action to help resolve an issue.			
I can explain the possible consequences of taking action to help resolve a national or global issue.			

Prior learning

1 Work with a partner or in a small group. Look at the picture your teacher shows you. What might the issues be?

a ....

b ....

c ....

d ....

2 Do your classmates agree with you?
Make any changes to your list of issues in a different colour.

The topic I am working on today is …

....

> **Tip**
>
> When considering actions to help resolve issues, ask yourself: 'What is the issue?'; 'Why is the issue important?'; 'Who does the issue affect?'; 'When is action needed?'; 'Which resources do I need in order to take action?'; 'How will I know if my action is effective?'

Starter activity

1 Read the text your teacher gives you. Discuss it with a partner, then answer the questions:

a What is the issue? ....

b How has the issue arisen? ....

....

c Who does the issue involve? ....

d Which perspectives are given? ....

....

e How might the issue be resolved? ....

....

f What might be the possible consequences of resolving the issue at a personal, national and global level?

Personal ....

Local ....

Global ....

> **Tip**
>
> Courses of action need to be realistic; for example, giving a presentation to help raise awareness to make a positive difference to an issue.

Peer feedback

2 Share your answers from task 1 with another pair.

a Did they get all the same answers as you?

....

b If not, how did their answers differ?

....

....

c Why do you think this was?

....

d Do you think you need to make any changes to your answers? Why?

....

....

> **Tip**
>
> There may be many different actions that can help make a positive difference to an issue. Choose one most suitable for the issue.

Main activity

1 Choose one of the issues your teacher has given you and complete the table.

Question (issue)		
Possible action	**Reasons for/against**	**Other factors** (e.g. who to involve, resources needed)
1		
2		
3		

Class discussion

2 Using what you've learnt from discussion with your partner and in the class discussion about courses of action, decide on your best possible course of action to help resolve your chosen issue and give reasons for your choice.

Course of action: ....

....

Reasons for this choice: ....

....

Independent reflection activity

Do you think it might now be easier for you to come up with different types of action to help resolve issues?

....

....

Why?

....

....

As well as analysis skills, which other skills have you used today?

....

....

Check your learning

If you haven't already done so, complete the **How will I know if I reach my goals?** table with 'Not there yet' or 'Achieved'. Don't forget to add examples from your challenge.

5

Developing analysis skills: Lesson 5

2.2 Identify patterns and trends in graphical or numerical data in order to support an argument

2.3 Make some links between causes and consequences of an issue at personal, local and global levels

My learning goals are to develop my knowledge and understanding about:

- using patterns and trends in graphical data to support an argument
- the causes/consequences of an issue at a personal, local or global level

How will I know if I reach my goals?

As you work through this lesson, tick the 'Achieved' box to show you have achieved your learning goals. If you haven't quite achieved your learning goals, tick 'Not there yet'. Start to think about how you are going to show your learning goals in your challenge. Add an example from your challenge once you have achieved each learning goal.

Lesson 5	Not there yet	Achieved	Example
I can identify a pattern/trend in a graph and recognise how this can support an argument.			
I can explain some causes/consequences of an issue at a personal, local or global level.			

Prior learning

1 Discuss with a partner. Answer the following questions:

a What is meant by the term 'evidence' in Global Perspectives?

....

....

....

b What types of evidence can you include when exploring the causes, consequences and perspectives of an issue?

....

....

....

Class discussion

2 Discuss your ideas with your classmates. Add any further ideas to your responses for task 1 in a different colour.

The topic I am working on today is …

....

Starter activity

Look at the graph your teacher shows you.

1 What is the graph about?

....

2 What is the pattern/trend in the graph?

....

3 What argument might the evidence in the graph help support?

....

4 What do you find interesting about the evidence in the graph?

……………………………………………………………………………………………

Do your classmates agree? Yes/No

> **Tip**
>
> Explaining reasons/causes and consequences at a personal level means explaining what they mean to an individual; for example, the reason you might play football is because you enjoy it and you can play with friends. A consequence for you is that you get fitter.

Main activity

1 Look at the issue your teacher gives you and discuss it in your team.

2 Complete the table.

Issue		
1	Causes/reasons at a personal level	
2	Consequences at a personal level	
3	Causes/reasons at a local level	
4	Consequences at a local level	
5	Causes/reasons at a global level	
6	Consequences at a global level	
	Information sources	

> **Tip**
>
> Explaining reasons/causes and consequences at a local level means explaining what they mean to the local community; for example, the reason football is a popular sport is that it's fun and doesn't cost much to play in the streets or parks. A consequence is it that it brings people together to support their local team.

Independent reflection activity

What helped you to learn today?

....

....

....

How did you help someone else learn today?

....

....

....

Tip

Evidence is the available body of facts or information showing whether something is true.

Check your learning

If you haven't already done so, complete the **How will I know if I reach my goals?** table with 'Not there yet' or 'Achieved'. Don't forget to add examples from your challenge.

Tip

Explaining reasons/causes and consequences at a global level means explaining what they mean to the whole world; for example, as football is such a popular sport globally, there are events such as the World Cup and, as a consequence, supporters can get a sense of national pride and global unity during these events.

6

Developing analysis skills: Lesson 6

2.1 Identify perspectives and synthesise arguments and evidence from a range of sources on a given topic

My learning goals are to develop my knowledge and understanding about:

- the difference between a global, a national and a personal perspective
- identifying and explaining different perspectives
- synthesising arguments and evidence related to a perspective

How will I know if I reach my goals?

As you work through this lesson, tick the 'Achieved' box to show you have achieved your learning goals. If you haven't quite achieved your learning goals, tick 'Not there yet'. Start to think about how you are going to show your learning goals in your challenge. Add an example from your challenge once you have achieved each learning goal.

Lesson 6	Not there yet	Achieved	Example
I understand the difference between a global, a national and a personal perspective.			
I can identify and explain some different perspectives.			
I can synthesise some arguments and evidence related to a perspective.			

Prior learning

1 Think about the topic you worked on in the Main activity of Lesson 5 to develop your skills. Complete these sentence starters:

I used to think ....

Now I think ....

because ....

2 Share your thinking with your partner. Has your partner's thinking changed or developed? How?

....

....

3 Is what you think considered as a global, national or personal perspective?

....

The topic I am working on today is ...

....

Starter activity

1 Look at the picture your teacher shows you. Discuss it with a partner. How might the picture represent a global, a national and a personal perspective?

Global ....

National ....

Personal ....

2 Using what you've learnt from discussion about perspectives, tell your partner what you think the difference is between a global, a national and a personal perspective.

....

....

Tip

A global perspective may come from a specific country, organisation, institution or even an individual, but it will have influence that spreads beyond any one country.

3 Do you think your partner understands the difference between a global, national and a personal perspective? Yes/No

If not, how can you help them to understand the difference?

....

....

Tip

You must support a perspective with evidence and sources of information.

Main activity

1 Look at the sub-topic your teacher shows you. Find some ideas and evidence for each of the perspectives in the table below. Discuss them with a partner, then make notes in the table.

Sub-topic	
Global perspective	
National perspective	
References	

Tip

For a perspective to be personal, it must be based on evidence. Otherwise, it is just an opinion.

Tip

To synthesise means to bring together ideas from different sources to present an argument or develop a perspective.

2 Choose one of the perspectives from task 1. Write a short paragraph to explain the arguments and evidence related to your chosen perspective.

Perspective: ....

....

....

....

Independent reflection activity

1 Using what you have learnt so far, are you developing your understanding of the following?

a A global perspective Yes/No

b A national perspective Yes/No

c A personal perspective Yes/No

2 Give an example for each.

a A global perspective ....

b A national perspective ....

c A personal perspective ....

3 What do you now need to do to develop your understanding further?

....

....

....

Check your learning

If you haven't already done so, complete the **How will I know if I reach my goals?** table with 'Not there yet' or 'Achieved'. Don't forget to add examples from your challenge.

Self-assessment 2

Look back at self-assessment 1. How much further progress do you feel you have made so far in developing your analysis skills?

For each learning objective in the table below, shade in the response that matches yours most closely. Give one example for this response. Eventually, you are aiming for green!

Learning objectives: *to develop my knowledge and understanding about how to …*	RED	AMBER	GREEN
2.1 Identify perspectives and synthesise arguments and evidence from a range of sources on a given topic.	I can identify different perspectives with help. I can synthesise some arguments and evidence with help.	I can identify different perspectives. I can synthesise some arguments and evidence.	I can identify different perspectives. I can synthesise some arguments and evidence. I can help others synthesise arguments and evidence.
2.2 Identify patterns and trends in graphical or numerical data in order to support an argument.	I can identify patterns/trends from a graph with help. I can explain how the information in graphs can be used as evidence to support an argument with help.	I can identify patterns/trends from a graph. I can explain how the information in graphs can be used as evidence to support an argument.	I can identify patterns/ trends from a graph. I can explain how the information in graphs can be used as evidence to support an argument. I can help others identify patterns and trends from a graph.
2.3 Make some links between causes and consequences of an issue at personal, local and global levels.	I can explain some of the causes or consequences of an issue at different levels (personal, local, global) with help. I can make some links between causes and consequences at different levels with help.	I can explain the causes or consequences of an issue at different levels (personal, local, global). I can make some links between causes and consequences at different levels.	I can explain the causes or consequences of an issue at different levels (personal, local, global). I can make some links between causes and consequences at different levels (global, national, personal). I can help others understand how to make links between causes and consequences at different levels.

Continued

Learning objectives: *to develop my knowledge and understanding about how to …*	RED	AMBER	GREEN
2.4 Recommend an appropriate course of action and explain possible consequences for a national or global issue.	I can suggest at least one action to make a positive difference to an issue with help. I can explain the possible consequences of this action with help.	I can suggest at least one action to make a positive difference to an issue. I can explain the consequences of this action for a global or national issue.	I can suggest actions to make a positive difference to an issue. I can explain the consequences of these actions for a global or national issue.

Examples:

2.1 ....

2.2 ....

2.3 ....

2.4 ....

Reflect on your responses in your self-assessment and identify two areas for improvement. Set yourself two learning targets – how you will improve upon the two areas. For example, 'I will try to help others understand how to make connections between the causes of or reasons for an issue at different levels.'

Learning targets:

1 Area for improvement: ....

How I will improve: ....

2 Area for improvement: ....

How I will improve: ....

Challenge topic review

Think about the challenge topic you have been exploring and complete the following statements.

I was surprised to discover that ....

....

I didn't know ....

....

I now think ....

....

7

Getting better at analysis skills: Lesson 7

2.1 Identify perspectives and synthesise arguments and evidence from a range of sources on a given topic

My learning goals are to get better at:

- understanding Global Perspectives key terms
- explaining the perspectives of different groups of stakeholders
- synthesising arguments and evidence from different information sources

How will I know if I reach my goals?

As you work through this lesson, tick the 'Achieved' box to show you have achieved your learning goals. If you haven't quite achieved your learning goals, tick 'Not there yet'. Start to think about how you are going to show your learning goals in your challenge. Add an example from your challenge once you have achieved each learning goal.

Lesson 7	Not there yet	Achieved	Example
I understand Global Perspectives key terms.			
I can explain the perspectives of different groups of stakeholders.			
I can synthesise arguments and evidence from different sources.			

Prior learning

Answer the quick quiz questions your teacher gives you.

1 ....

....

2 ....

....

3 ....

....

4 ....

....

5 ....

....

Starter activity

Class discussion

1 After class discussion about answers to the questions in the Prior learning activity, write down all five questions and answers.

1 ....

....

2 ....

....

3 ....

....

Tip

An argument is a reason or set of reasons given in support of an idea, action or perspective.

Tip

Evidence is the available facts or information showing the truth of an argument.

4 ....

....

5 ....

....

2 Discuss the list with a partner. Write down five further questions with answers.

1 ....

....

2 ....

....

3 ....

....

4 ....

....

5 ....

....

3 Ask your questions to another pair to check they know the answers.

Did they get all the answers to the questions right? Yes/No

Which one(s) did they get wrong?

....

Why do you think this was?

....

Tip

A group of people who share common knowledge and values that influence their perspective are called stakeholders.

Tip

A stakeholder is someone with a vested interested in a topic/issue. The topic/issue affects them somehow.

Main activity

The topic I am working on today is …

....

> **Tip**
>
> There will be different perspectives within a group of stakeholders. For example, learners could make up a group of stakeholders, but it is likely that learners in Grade 7 will have a different perspective about a topic to learners in Grade 9.

1 In teams, look at the issue your teacher shows you. Write the issue in the middle of the diagram. Brainstorm all the groups of people (stakeholders) who might have an interest in this issue. Add as many circles and arrows to the diagram as you need to record your ideas.

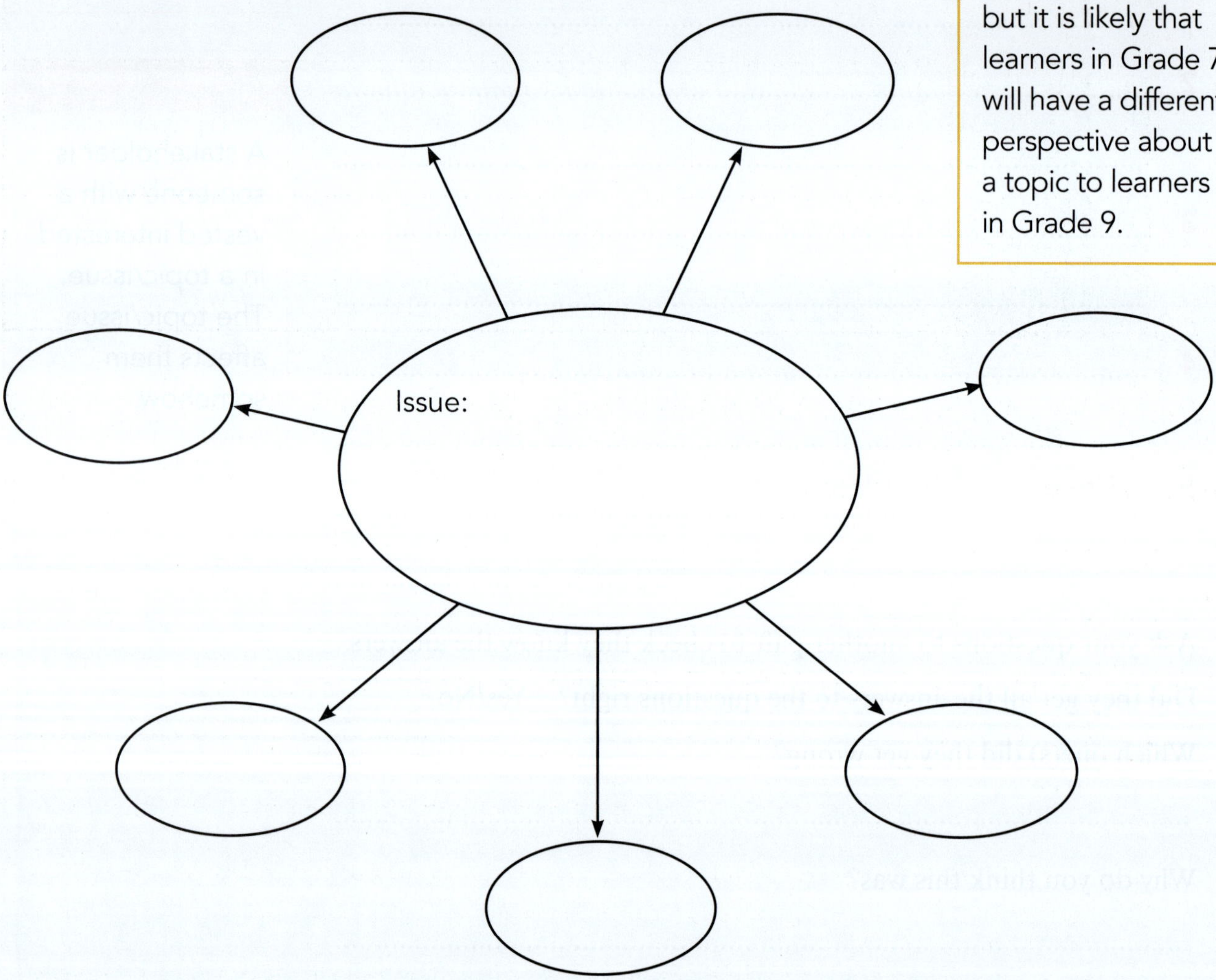

2 a In your team, choose one group of stakeholders from your diagram.

....

b Discuss your chosen group of stakeholders and do some research. Make notes on the arguments and evidence to support the perspective of your stakeholders. Complete the table.

Stakeholder group	
Perspective	
Argument(s)	
Evidence	
References	

Independent reflection activity

What skills have you improved today?

....

....

What skill do you still need to improve on and how are you going to do this?

....

....

....

Check your learning

If you haven't already done so, complete the **How will I know if I reach my goals?** table with 'Not there yet' or 'Achieved'. Don't forget to add examples from your challenge.

8

Getting better at analysis skills: Lesson 8

2.1 Identify perspectives and synthesise arguments and evidence from a range of sources on a given topic

2.2 Identify patterns and trends in graphical or numerical data in order to support an argument

My learning goals are to get better at:

- explaining who the stakeholders are for a specific issue
- synthesising arguments and evidence from different sources to support a perspective
- understanding how numerical data can be used as evidence to support an argument

How will I know if I reach my goals?

As you work through this lesson, tick the 'Achieved' box to show you have achieved your learning goals. If you haven't quite achieved your learning goals, tick 'Not there yet'. Start to think about how you are going to show your learning goals in your challenge. Add an example from your challenge once you have achieved each learning goal.

Lesson 8	Not there yet	Achieved	Example
I can explain who the stakeholders are for a specific issue.			
I can synthesise arguments and evidence from different sources to support a perspective.			
I understand how numerical data can be used as evidence to support an argument.			

Prior learning

1 What do you now understand by the term 'stakeholder'? Discuss it with a partner. Write a definition in your own words.

A stakeholder is ....

2 Give three examples of stakeholders for the issue you worked on in the Main activity in Lesson 7.

a ....

b ....

c ....

3 Choose one of the groups of stakeholders in task **2**. Discuss these stakeholders with a partner. Explain why you think they are stakeholders for the issue.

....

....

The topic I am working on today is …

....

Starter activity

1 Look at the line graph your teacher shows you. Write down and answer the questions your teacher gives you.

1 ....

....

2 ....

....

3 ....

....

Tip

When trying to deepen your understanding of an issue, you need to look for groups of stakeholders who are like to have different perspectives.

4 ....

....

5 ....

....

6 ....

....

7 ....

....

8 ....

....

9 ....

....

10 ....

....

> **Tip**
> Patterns/trends in line graphs are likely to show fluctuations; for example, a rise/increase, a fall/decrease, or no change at all.

> **Tip**
> Patterns/trends in line graphs might show the difference between two groups; for example, the difference in opinions between men and women or a difference in quantity between two different countries.

Class discussion

2 After class discussion about the questions and answers in task 1, make any changes to your answers in a different colour.

Main activity

1 Refer to your notes from the Main activity in Lesson 7. In your team, write the first draft of an email or blog to present your chosen stakeholders' perspective on the issue. Write on a separate sheet of paper.

> **Tip**
> When writing an email or blog, always think of who you are writing to/for as well as what you are writing about.

Independent reflection activity

What did you find easy in today's lesson?

....

....

What did you need help with in today's lesson?

....

....

Check your learning

If you haven't already done so, complete the **How will I know if I reach my goals?** table with 'Not there yet' or 'Achieved'. Don't forget to add examples from your challenge.

9

Getting better at analysis skills: Lesson 9

2.1 Identify perspectives and synthesise arguments and evidence from a range of sources on a given topic

2.3 Make some links between causes and consequences of an issue at personal, local and global levels

2.4 Recommend an appropriate course of action and explain possible consequences for a national or global issue

My learning goals are to get better at:

- identifying and explaining perspectives, arguments and evidence
- making links between causes and consequences of an issue
- suggesting an appropriate course of action for a national or global issue and explaining the possible consequences of this course of action

How will I know if I reach my goals?

As you work through this lesson, tick the 'Achieved' box to show you have achieved your learning goals. If you haven't quite achieved your learning goals, tick 'Not there yet'. Start to think about how you are going to show your learning goals in your challenge. Add an example from your challenge once you have achieved each learning goal.

Lesson 9	Not there yet	Achieved	Example
I can identify and explain perspectives, arguments and evidence.			
I can make links between causes and consequences of an issue.			
I can suggest an appropriate course of action for a national or global issue and explain the possible consequences of this course of action.			

Prior learning

In your team, discuss your draft email/blog from Lesson 8. Answer the following questions.

1 What have you identified as the causes of your issue?

....

....

2 What have you identified as the consequences of your issue?

....

....

3 What other causes of your issue can you think of?

....

....

4 What other consequences of your issue can you think of?

....

....

Continued

5 Are there any links between the causes and consequences of your issue? If so, what are they?

....

....

The topic I am working on today is …

....

> **Tip**
>
> A course of action needs an outcome; for example, a presentation, leaflet or poster promoting something or raising awareness about something to help make a positive difference.

Starter activity

Peer feedback

Swap your email/blog from Lesson 8 with another team. Give feedback on the other team's email/blog, answering the following questions. Give details.

1 Is it clear who the stakeholder group is? Yes/No

....

2 Is it clear what the issue is? Yes/No

....

3 Is it clear what the perspective is? Yes/No

....

4 Is the email/blog focused on the issue? Yes/No

....

5 Does the email/blog contain at least two arguments? Yes/No

....

6 Is each argument supported by at least one piece of evidence? Yes/No

....

7 Is each piece of evidence referenced in the reference list? Yes/No

....

> **Tip**
>
> Courses of action need to be realistic. This means you need to explain how it will work to help resolve or make a positive difference to an issue.

8 Does the email/blog start and end in an appropriate way? Yes/No

....

9 One highlight:

....

10 One area for improvement:

....

Main activity

1 As a team, use the feedback gained in the Starter activity to improve your email/blog.

2 If necessary, do further research on your issue from the perspective of your stakeholder group.

3 Discuss the issue and possible courses of action to help make a positive difference or resolve the issue. Then make notes below.

a Course of action:

....

b Reason(s) for this course of action:

....

....

c Possible consequences of this course of action:

....

....

d Notes from research to include in the email/blog:

....

....

....

....

Tip

A course of action needs to be related to an issue and help meet an aim. For example, if the aim is to raise awareness about something, appropriate courses of action might be to create a presentation, a leaflet or a poster.

Tip

An example for a local course of action might be to raise awareness about the links between social media and mental health issues amongst young people. An outcome to do this might be a presentation to classmates in school.

Independent reflection activity

What skills have you used in today's lesson?

....

....

How might you further develop these skills?

....

....

Check your learning

If you haven't already done so, complete the **How will I know if I reach my goals?** table with 'Not there yet' or 'Achieved'. Don't forget to add examples from your challenge.

Self-assessment 3

Look back at self-assessments 1 and 2. How much further progress do you feel you have made so far in developing your analysis skills?

For each learning objective in the table below, shade in the response that matches yours most closely. Give one example for this response. Eventually, you are aiming for green!

Learning objectives: *to get better at understanding how to …*	RED	AMBER	GREEN
2.1 Identify perspectives and synthesise arguments and evidence from a range of sources on a given topic.	I know some key Global Perspectives terms. I can explain the perspective of a group of stakeholders with help. I can synthesise some arguments and evidence with help.	I know some key Global Perspectives terms. I can explain the perspective of a group of stakeholders. I can synthesise some arguments and evidence.	I know key Global Perspectives terms. I can explain the perspective of a group of stakeholders. I can synthesise some arguments and evidence from different information sources. I can help others synthesise arguments and evidence from different information sources.

Continued

Learning objectives: *to get better at understanding how to …*	RED	AMBER	GREEN
2.2 Identify patterns and trends in graphical or numerical data in order to support an argument.	I can identify patterns/trends from a graph with help. I can analyse a graph to gain some information with help. I can explain how the information in graphs can be used as evidence to support an argument with help.	I can identify patterns/trends from a graph. I can analyse a graph to gain some relevant information. I can explain how the information in graphs can be used as evidence to support an argument.	I can identify patterns/ trends from a graph. I can analyse a graph to gain relevant information. I can help others analyse a graph. I can explain how the information in graphs can be used as evidence to support an argument and help others understand this.
2.3 Make some links between causes and consequences of an issue at personal, local and global levels.	I can explain some of the causes or consequences of an issue with help. I can make some links between the causes and consequences of an issue with help.	I can explain the causes and consequences of an issue. I can make some links between the causes and consequences of an issue.	I can explain the causes and consequences of an issue. I can make links between the causes and consequences of an issue. I can help others recognise the links between the causes and consequences of an issue.
2.4 Recommend an appropriate course of action and explain possible consequences for a national or global issue.	I can suggest some courses of action to help resolve or make a positive difference to an issue with help. I can explain the possible consequences of these courses of action with help.	I can suggest some courses of action to help resolve or make a positive difference to an issue. I can explain the possible consequences of these courses of action.	I can suggest realistic courses of action to help resolve or make a positive difference to an issue. I can explain the possible consequences of these courses of action. I can help others suggest possible courses of action and understand the possible consequences of these courses of action.

Continued

Examples:

2.1 ....

2.2 ....

2.3 ....

2.4 ....

Reflect on your responses in your self-assessment and identify two areas for improvement. Set yourself two learning targets – how you will improve upon the two areas. For example, 'I will try to help others understand the difference between a global and national perspective'.

Learning targets:

1 Area for improvement: ....

How I will improve: ....

2 Area for improvement: ....

How I will improve: ....

Challenge topic review

Think about the challenge topic you have been exploring and complete the following statements.

I was surprised to discover that ....

....

I didn't know ....

....

I now think ....

....

Section 3

Evaluation

This section of your Learner's Skills Book 9 helps you to develop your evaluation skills using interesting global topics.

Starting with . . .

As you start to develop your evaluation skills in Stage 9, you will be explaining how evaluation and analysis in Global Perspectives differ, as well as the difference between real and fake news and how to recognise both. You will also evaluate a range of different information sources to check their reliability, if they contain bias and determine how effective they are in terms of the argument(s) they present.

Developing . . .

As you further develop your evaluation skills in Stage 9, you will be evaluating the reasoning in arguments, which also includes recognising and explaining counterarguments. You will develop your knowledge and understanding about claims, about reasoning to justify claims and about evidence in support of claims. You will explore bias and explain why some sources may be biased. You will also consider the purpose of different information sources and the audience for different information sources.

Getting better at . . .

As you get better at evaluating in Stage 9, you will continue to evaluate different information sources in terms of their argument and how effective that is, and continue to reflect on and evaluate the reliability of information sources, considering any bias they might contain. You will continue to explore the difference between the purpose of information sources and who a source is aimed at. You will also be able to explain the difference between fact and opinion, and give examples of each of these types of evidence.

1

Starting with evaluation skills: Lesson 1

3.1 Evaluate a range of sources, considering the author and purpose and how well they are supported by other sources, explaining why some may be biased

My learning goals are to start to:

- explain how evaluation and analysis in Global Perspectives differ
- understand the difference between real news and fake news, and know how to recognise both

How will I know if I reach my goals?

As you work through this lesson, tick the 'Achieved' box to show you have achieved your learning goals. If you haven't quite achieved your learning goals, tick 'Not there yet'. Start to think about how you are going to show your learning goals in your challenge. Add an example from your challenge once you have achieved each learning goal.

Lesson 1	Not there yet	Achieved	Example
I can explain how evaluation and analysis in Global Perspectives differ.			
I understand the difference between real news and fake news, and know how to recognise both.			

Prior learning

1 Discuss these questions with a partner. Then write down the answers.

a In Global Perspectives, which of these words relate to analysis and which relate to evaluation?

strengths	causes	highlights	improvements	reasons
actions	judgement	weaknesses	perspectives	consequences

Analysis: ....

Evaluation: ....

b If asked to analyse something in Global Perspectives lessons, what would you be doing?

....

c If asked to evaluate something in Global Perspectives lessons, what would you be doing?

....

....

2 Share your ideas with your classmates. After class discussion about analysis and evaluation, explain the difference.

....

....

Starter activity

1 Which one of the following statements is not evaluation?

A The evidence is strong

B It is a bit outdated as it was written in 2013

C The argument cites expert views

D The article is biased because the author is a government minister

Tip

To cite something means to refer to a text, book or author as evidence to help support an argument.

E It is a balanced argument

F This is due to improvements in communication

G Numerical data supports the argument

Share your ideas to see if your classmates agree.

2 Are you becoming more confident in knowing what the term 'evaluation' means and how it differs from analysis? Yes/No

3 How are you going to develop this confidence further?

....

The topic I am working on today is ...

....

Main activity

1 Discuss the following questions with a partner. Then write down the answers.

a What is the difference between real news and fake news?

....

b Why do you think fake news is created?

....

....

c Why do you think it's important to recognise fake news?

....

d Do you think that your teacher generally gives you fake news items? Yes/No

Why/Why not?

....

Tip

Bias is a judgement based on a personal point of view. People who are biased often believe what they want to believe, refusing to take different perspectives or the opinions of others into consideration.

Tip

A one-sided argument does not present all the evidence; for example, citing the advantages of growing up bilingual but not the disadvantages.

Tip

A balanced argument is one where both sides are discussed equally.

2 Look at the news item your teacher shows you. Discuss it with a partner.

a Do you think the news item is real or fake?

....

b Why do you think this?

....

....

> **Tip**
>
> Strong evidence is evidence that comes from well-known sources such as the United Nations or the World Health Organization.

Peer feedback

3 Do your classmates agree? Yes/No

a What do they disagree with? ....

b Why do you think this is?

....

c Might you change your answers to task 2 as a result of peer feedback? Why?

....

> **Tip**
>
> When evaluating a news item, try to give reasons why you think it might be real or fake.

Class discussion

4 After class discussion about the questions, write down what to look for to be able to judge if a news item is real or fake.

....

....

....

> **Tip**
>
> To evaluate a source, you need to give its strengths and weaknesses.

> **Tip**
>
> The term 'fake news' is given to false information that is deliberately created to trick people into believing it is true and is often created for political or business reasons.

> **Tip**
>
> To judge if a news item is real, search for it in different information sources.

Independent reflection activity

Which part of today's lesson did you find the most difficult?

....

....

Why do you think this was?

....

....

How are you going to get better at this?

....

....

Check your learning

If you haven't already done so, complete the **How will I know if I reach my goals?** table with 'Not there yet' or 'Achieved'. Don't forget to add examples from your challenge.

2

Starting with evaluation skills: Lesson 2

3.1 Evaluate a range of sources, considering the author and purpose and how well they are supported by other sources, explaining why some may be biased

My learning goals are to start to:

- explain the reliability of information sources
- describe the bias in information sources

How will I know if I reach my goals?

As you work through this lesson, tick the 'Achieved' box to show you have achieved your learning goals. If you haven't quite achieved your learning goals, tick 'Not there yet'. Start to think about how you are going to show your learning goals in your challenge. Add an example from your challenge once you have achieved each learning goal.

Lesson 2	Not there yet	Achieved	Example
I can explain the reliability of an information source.			
I can describe the bias in information sources.			

Prior learning

1 How can you tell if a news item is real or fake? Discuss with a partner.

a Real:

....

....

b Fake:

....

....

2 Share your ideas with another pair. Do they have the same ideas as you? Add further ideas in a different colour.

3 Using what you have learnt from class discussion about real and fake news, complete the following statement:

The difference between real and fake news is ....

....

....

The topic I am working on today is …

....

Starter activity

1 Look at the information source your teacher gives you. Discuss it with a partner. How reliable do you think this information source is? Why?

....

....

....

Use the checklist to help you determine its reliability.

	Checklist	Yes/No	Notes (e.g. type of evidence; who wrote/published the source; any bias?)
1	Are the arguments in the information source supported by evidence?		
2	Have you heard of the author/ organisation that published the information source?		
3	Does the information source look real?		
4	Is the evidence to support the arguments strong?		
5	Does the information source sound believable?		
6	Is the author of the information source a real person?		
7	Is there anything odd about the information source?		
8	Is the information presented free from bias?		

....

....

....

....

Tip

A reliable source is one that provides a detailed, well-reasoned argument, analysis or discussion that is supported by strong evidence.

Class discussion

2 Using what you have learnt from class discussion about source reliability, how else might you check the reliability of the information source in task 1?

....

....

Main activity

1 Look at the issue your teacher gives you.

a Write down the issue.

....

b Work with a partner. Find an information source related to this issue and write down the reference.

....

c Read the information source and note the main ideas.

....

....

d Do you think the information source is reliable? Yes/No

Why?

....

e Do you think the information source contains bias/is biased? Yes/No

Why?

....

2 Share your information source with another pair. Do they think it contains bias/is biased? Why?

....

3 Check with your teacher if the information source contains bias/is biased.

....

Tip

To check if a source is reliable, check the author, the date and the evidence presented in support of the argument(s).

Tip

To check a source for bias, look to see if the information presented is one-sided or focused only on the author's opinion.

Tip

A biased author may not present all the facts or develop a reasoned argument to support their opinion(s). For example, someone in favour of technological advancement is unlikely to give the disadvantages of digital technologies.

Independent reflection activity

Which part of this lesson did you enjoy most? Why?

....

....

....

How have you used research skills today?

....

....

Check your learning

If you haven't already done so, complete the **How will I know if I reach my goals?** table with 'Not there yet' or 'Achieved'. Don't forget to add examples from your challenge.

3

Starting with evaluation skills: Lesson 3

3.1 Evaluate a range of sources, considering the author and purpose and how well they are supported by other sources, explaining why some may be biased

3.2 Evaluate the reasoning of an argument in a source, considering the structure and techniques used

My learning goals are to start to:

- explain the reliability of information sources
- explain the effectiveness of information sources in terms of the argument(s) they present

How will I know if I reach my goals?

As you work through this lesson, tick the 'Achieved' box to show you have achieved your learning goals. If you haven't quite achieved your learning goals, tick 'Not there yet'. Start to think about how you are going to show your learning goals in your challenge. Add an example from your challenge once you have achieved each learning goal.

Lesson 3	Not there yet	Achieved	Example
I know how to check and explain the reliability of an information source.			
I can explain how effective a source is in terms of its argument(s).			

Prior learning

1 How might you check if an information source is reliable? Discuss with a partner.

....

....

2 Share with another pair. Do they agree or have different ideas?
Add further ideas in a different colour.

....

....

The topic I am working on today is …

....

Starter activity

1 Look at the video clip your teacher shows you. Complete the checklist.

	Checklist	Yes/No	**Notes** (e.g. type of evidence; who published the source; any bias?)
1	Are the arguments in the information source supported by evidence?		
2	Have you heard of the author/ organisation that published the information source?		
3	Does the information source look real?		
4	Is the evidence to support the arguments strong?		
5	Does the information source sound believable?		
6	Is the author of the information source a real person?		

	Checklist	Yes/No	Notes (e.g. type of evidence; who published the source; any bias?)
7	Is there anything odd about the information source?		
8	Is the information presented free from bias?		

2 Discuss your ideas with a partner.

How reliable do you think this information source is? Why?

....

....

....

3 Share with another pair. Do they agree with you and your partner? Yes/No

Why? ....

Main activity

1 Look at the information source your teacher shows you. Work with a partner to find the story in the information source. Make notes about the main idea and the facts.

Main idea: ....

Facts: ....

....

....

2 Complete the checklist, expanding on your answers in the Notes column.

	Checklist	Yes/No	Notes (e.g. where else reported; purpose; why believable; why logical; author's expertise; date; type of evidence, etc.)
1	Has the story been reported anywhere else?		
2	Is the purpose of the story clear?		
3	Have you heard of the organisation that published the story?		
4	Does the story sound believable?		
5	Is the argument in the story logical?		
6	Are there any errors in spelling or grammar (in text only)?		
7	Is the author of the story a real person?		
8	Is there anything odd about the date the story was published?		
9	Does the story contain bias?		
10	Is there any other evidence to support the story?		

3 **a** Do you think this information source is reliable? ....

b Why? ....

....

4 **a** Do you think the source is effective in terms of the argument(s) it presents?

....

b Why?

....

Tip

A reliable source of information is a source that can be trusted to be true.

Class discussion

5 Discuss as a class. What have your classmates found when checking for the reliability and effectiveness of information sources?

a Reliability:

....

....

b Effectiveness:

....

....

6 a Using what you have learnt from class discussion about reliable information sources, do you feel more confident about judging if an information source is reliable? Why?

Yes, because ....

No, because ....

b What would help you further?

....

7 a Using what you have learnt from class discussion about effective information sources in terms of the argument(s) they present, do you feel more confident about judging if an information source is effective? Why?

Yes, because ....

No, because ....

b What would help you further?

....

Tip

Bias is prejudice for or against something or someone generally in a way considered to be unfair.

Tip

An unreliable source is a source that cannot be trusted to be true.

Tip

It is most likely that you will have heard of the more reliable sources of information, for example, newspapers such as *The Guardian*, *Huffington Post* and *The Times of India*; news agencies such as the BBC, CNN and Al Jazeera, and global organisations such as the United Nations and the World Wide Fund for Nature (WWF).

Tip

An effective information source has a logical argument that makes sense and is supported with reasoning and evidence. To judge if an information source is effective, you need to be persuaded by the argument(s) it makes.

Tip

Most information sources contain some form of bias. You need to decide whether any reported facts are examples of bias or are fake. For example, it is a fact that 'a politician was at a conference', but a news story that reports he was there to support a policy when he actually said that he opposes the policy is untrue and therefore fake news. Such a news story is also an example of political bias on the part of the author.

Independent reflection activity

What skills have you used today?

....

....

What has helped you to learn today?

....

....

Check your learning

If you haven't already done so, complete the **How will I know if I reach my goals?** table with 'Not there yet' or 'Achieved'. Don't forget to add examples from your challenge.

Self-assessment 1

How much progress do you feel you have made so far in developing your evaluation skills?

For each learning objective in the table below, shade in the response that matches yours most closely. Give one example for this response. Eventually, you are aiming for green!

Learning objectives: *to start to …*	RED	AMBER	GREEN
3.1 Evaluate a range of sources, considering the author and purpose and how well they are supported by other sources, explaining why some may be biased.	I can explain the difference between analysis and evaluation in Global Perspectives with help. I can explain the reliability of some information sources with help. I understand the difference between real and fake news, and I can recognise both with help. I can describe some bias in an information source with help.	I can explain the difference between analysis and evaluation in Global Perspectives. I can explain the reliability of some information sources. I understand the difference between real and fake news, and I can recognise both. I can describe some bias in an information source.	I can explain the difference between analysis and evaluation in Global Perspectives. I can explain the reliability of some information sources. I understand the difference between real and fake news, and I can recognise both. I can describe bias in an information source. I can help others judge the reliability of information sources and check information sources for bias.
3.2 Evaluate the reasoning of an argument in a source, considering the structure and techniques used.	I can explain the effectiveness of a source in terms of its argument(s) with help.	I can explain the effectiveness of a source in terms of its argument(s).	I can explain the effectiveness of a source in terms of its argument(s). I can help others judge the effectiveness of a source in terms of its argument(s).

Continued

Examples:

3.1 ....

3.2 ....

Reflect on your responses in your self-assessment and identify two areas for improvement. Set yourself two learning targets – how you will improve upon the two areas. For example, 'I will check that the information sources I use are up-to-date.'

Learning targets:

1 Area for improvement: ....

How I will improve: ....

2 Area for improvement: ....

How I will improve: ....

Challenge topic review

Think about the challenge topic you have been exploring and complete the following statements.

I was surprised to discover that ....

....

I didn't know ....

....

I now think ....

....

4

Developing evaluation skills: Lesson 4

3.2 Evaluate the reasoning of an argument in a source, considering the structure and techniques used

My learning goals are to develop my knowledge and understanding about:

- evaluating the reasoning of an argument in an information source
- recognising counterarguments in information sources

How will I know if I reach my goals?

As you work through this lesson, tick the 'Achieved' box to show you have achieved your learning goals. If you haven't quite achieved your learning goals, tick 'Not there yet'. Start to think about how you are going to show your learning goals in your challenge. Add an example from your challenge once you have achieved each learning goal.

Lesson 4	Not there yet	Achieved	Example
I can evaluate the reasoning of an argument in an information source.			
I can recognise a counterargument in an information source.			

Prior learning

1 Which of the following describes an argument in Global Perspectives? Discuss this with a partner.

A A heated exchange of opposite viewpoints or opinions, often without supported reasoning or evidence

B A reason or reasons given in support of an idea, perspective or course of action

....

Do your classmates agree? Yes/No

Why? ....

2 Using what you have learnt from class discussion about arguments, explain the features of an effective argument to someone who doesn't know what you do in Global Perspectives lessons.

An effective argument ....

....

The topic I am working on today is …

....

Starter activity

Look at the picture your teacher shows you.

1 Write down three claims related to the picture.

a ....

b ....

c ....

2 After discussion with your classmates, write down three further claims.

d ....

e ....

f ....

3 Using what you've learnt from giving examples of claims, how do you explain to someone else what a claim is?

A claim is ....

....

Peer feedback

4 Does your partner have the same ideas or further ideas? Add to your ideas in a different colour.

Main activity

1 Look at the text your teacher gives you. Discuss it with a partner and then answer the questions.

a What is the author's claim?

....

b What reasons and evidence does the author use to support their claim?

Reasons: ....

....

Evidence: ....

....

c What counterargument(s) is/are presented?

....

....

d Do you think the reasoning and evidence are strong?

Reasoning: Yes/No, because ....

....

Evidence: Yes/No, because ....

....

Tip

A claim is a statement or assertion that something is true, typically without providing supporting evidence or proof.

Tip

A claim answers the question: What do I think? For example, 'I think communication would be easier if we only had one language in the world.'

Tip

An argument in Global Perspectives is made up of a claim, the reasons for that claim and the evidence that supports that claim.

e Do you think the argument is effective? Yes/No
Why?/Why not?

....

....

Peer feedback

2 Check with another pair. Do they have the same answers as you? Yes/No

a Which skill do you need to develop (e.g. understanding what counterarguments are)?

....

b How are you going to do this?

....

Independent reflection activity

What skills have you used in today's lesson?

....

Do you feel more confident about telling someone what an effective argument is in Global Perspectives? Yes/No

How are you going to gain more confidence?

....

Complete this statement:

An effective argument in Global Perspectives ....

....

....

Check your learning

If you haven't already done so, complete the **How will I know if I reach my goals?** table with 'Not there yet' or 'Achieved'. Don't forget to add examples from your challenge.

Tip

A reason answers the question: Why do I think this? For example, ". . . because with too many languages, it becomes difficult to connect with each other and for businesses to trade with each other.'

Tip

Evidence answers the question: How do I know this? For example, 'A report in *The Telegraph* suggests everyone should learn at least one foreign language to broaden their perspective about the world.'

Tip

A counter-argument is a reason or set of reasons that oppose/go against an idea presented in an argument.

5

Developing evaluation skills: Lesson 5

3.2 Evaluate the reasoning of an argument in a source, considering the structure and techniques used

My learning goals are to develop my knowledge and understanding about:

- claims
- reasoning to justify claims
- evidence in support of claims
- counterarguments

How will I know if I reach my goals?

As you work through this lesson, tick the 'Achieved' box to show you have achieved your learning goals. If you haven't quite achieved your learning goals, tick 'Not there yet'. Start to think about how you are going to show your learning goals in your challenge. Add an example from your challenge once you have achieved each learning goal.

Lesson 5	Not there yet	Achieved	Example
I can explain what a claim is.			
I can justify a claim.			
I can give evidence in support of a claim.			
I can give an example of a counter argument.			

Prior learning

1 Which of these questions can you ask in order to identify a claim?

A How does the author know this?

B What does the author think?

C Why does the author think this?

....

Did you choose the same as your partner? Yes/No

2 What might you be able to identify by asking the other two questions in task 1?

....

....

3 Using what you've learnt from class discussion about claims, reasoning and evidence, give an example for each.

Claim: ....

Reason: ....

Evidence: ....

Starter activity

1 Watch the video clip your teacher shows you. Then write down:

a One claim in the video: ....

....

b Reason(s) for the claim: ....

....

c Evidence to support the claim: ....

....

2 Share your ideas with your partner. Do you think they understand what a claim, reasoning and evidence is?

Which do you think they need to develop their understanding of? Why?

....

Peer feedback

3 Check to see if your classmates have the same ideas. Add any further ideas in a different colour.

Main activity

1 Find an interesting text. Then write down:

a The text reference: ....

b One claim in the text: ....

....

c Reason(s) for the claim: ....

....

d One piece of evidence to support the claim: ....

....

e One counterargument: ....

....

f If the argument is effective and why: ....

....

Tip

Evidence is anything that can support or back up a claim; for example, a scientific report, a study or a quotation from someone or something that someone has read.

Tip

Reasons should justify the claim made; for example, the idea that it might be cheaper to buy other brands of chocolate does not justify the claim 'Everyone should eat Fairtrade chocolate'.

Peer feedback

2 Share your work with someone else. Give feedback by answering the questions. Then make changes to your own work if need be.

a Is the text reference correct? Yes/No

....

b Do you understand the claim? Yes/No

....

....

c Does the reasoning justify the claim? Yes/No

....

....

d Does the evidence support the claim? Yes/No

....

....

e Is a counterargument referred to? Yes/No

....

....

f Has a judgement been made about whether the argument is effective? Yes/No

....

....

Tip

A claim is often used as a headline for a news story; for example, 'More and more young people are now buying Fairtrade chocolate.'

Tip

An effective argument will include more than one claim with reasoning and supporting evidence.

Independent reflection activity

What helped you to learn today?

....

How did you help someone else learn today?

....

What skills have you used today?

....

Check your learning

If you haven't already done so, complete the **How will I know if I reach my goals?** table with 'Not there yet' or 'Achieved'. Don't forget to add examples from your challenge.

6

Developing analysis skills: Lesson 6

3.1 Evaluate a range of sources, considering the author and purpose and how well they are supported by other sources, explaining why some may be biased

My learning goals are to develop my knowledge and understanding about:

- bias, explaining why some sources may be biased
- the purpose of different information sources
- the audience for different information sources

How will I know if I reach my goals?

As you work through this lesson, tick the 'Achieved' box to show you have achieved your learning goals. If you haven't quite achieved your learning goals, tick 'Not there yet'. Start to think about how you are going to show your learning goals in your challenge. Add an example from your challenge once you have achieved each learning goal.

Lesson 6	Not there yet	Achieved	Example
I can explain why an information source may be biased.			
I can explain the purpose of different information sources.			
I can explain the audience for different information sources.			

Prior learning

1 What does the term 'bias' mean to you? Discuss it with a partner.

....

....

2 Share your definition of bias with another pair. Do they agree? Make changes to your definition in a different colour.

3 After class discussion, explain what bias is and give an example.

Bias is ....

....

An example of bias ....

....

Starter activity

1 Look at the information sources your teacher shows you. Discuss them with a partner. What is the purpose of each information source?

a ....

b ....

c ....

2 Are the information sources biased? Discuss with a partner. Explain your answer.

a ....

b ....

c ....

3 Do your classmates agree with your answers? Yes/No

If not, which answers do they disagree with? Why?

....

....

Class discussion

4 After class discussion about bias, explain why you think most information sources contain some form of bias.

....

....

Main activity

1 Look at the titles of different information sources your teacher shows you. Write them down.

A ....

B ....

C ....

2 Discuss the titles of the different information sources with a partner. Answer the following questions about each source:

a Which audience do you think each source is aimed at?

A ....

B ....

C ....

b What do you think is the purpose of each source?

A ....

B ....

C ....

c Do you think each source will contain bias? Why/Why not?

A ....

B ....

C ....

Tip

Bias is a judgement based on a personal point of view. People who are biased often believe what they want to believe, refusing to take different perspectives or the opinions of others into consideration.

Tip

Information sources may be biased for different reasons; for example, to persuade you of the value or importance of something.

Peer feedback

3 Share your answers to task **2** with another pair. Do they have other ideas you hadn't thought of? Add more ideas to your list in a different colour.

....

4 What do you now need to do to develop the skill of explaining the purpose of and audience for different information sources and identifying bias?

....

....

5 Using what you have learnt from class discussion, what do you think the titles of information sources can tell us?

....

....

Tip

Different information sources are created for different purposes. They can entertain, persuade, advise, argue, describe, inform or instruct; for example, an advertisement for a charity tries to persuade people to donate money to a good cause.

Tip

Different audiences are different groups of people; for example, of different ages or genders, students, parents, politicians, tourists, sports fans, the general public, etc.

Independent reflection activity

Think about your learning today. Complete these sentence stems:

I used to think ....

But now I think ....

Because ....

Has your partner's thinking changed or developed? Yes/No

How and why?

....

....

Check your learning

If you haven't already done so, complete the **How will I know if I reach my goals?** table with 'Not there yet' or 'Achieved'. Don't forget to add examples from your challenge.

Self-assessment 2

Look back at self-assessment 1. How much further progress do you feel you have made so far in developing your evaluation skills?

For each learning objective in the table below, shade in the response that matches yours most closely. Give one example for this response. Eventually, you are aiming for green!

Learning objectives: *to develop my knowledge and understanding about how to ...*	RED	AMBER	GREEN
3.1 Evaluate a range of sources, considering the author and purpose and how well they are supported by other sources, explaining why some may be biased.	I can explain what evaluation is. I can recognise if an information source contains bias with help. I can identify the audience for and purpose of different information sources with help.	I can explain what evaluation is. I can explain if an information source contains bias. I can identify the audience for and purpose of different information sources.	I can explain what evaluation is. I can explain if an information source contains bias. I can help others recognise bias in information sources. I can identify the audience for and purpose of different information sources. I can help others identify the audience for and purpose of different information sources.
3.2 Evaluate the reasoning of an argument in a source, considering the structure and techniques used,	I can evaluate the reasoning of an argument in an information source with help. I can recognise a counterargument with help.	I can evaluate the reasoning of an argument in an information source. I can recognise a counter-argument.	I can evaluate the reasoning of an argument in an information source. I can help others evaluate the reasoning of an argument. I can recognise a counterargument and can help others recognise counterarguments.

Continued

Examples:

3.1 ....

3.2 ....

Reflect on your responses in your self-assessment and identify two areas for improvement. Set yourself two learning targets – how you will improve upon the two areas. For example, 'I will check that I know what a counterargument is.'

Learning targets:

1 Area for improvement: ....

How I will improve: ....

2 Area for improvement: ....

How I will improve: ....

Challenge topic review

Think about the challenge topic you have been exploring and complete the following statements.

I was surprised to discover that ....

....

I didn't know ....

....

I now think ....

....

7

Getting better at evaluation skills: Lesson 7

3.1 Evaluate a range of sources, considering the author and purpose and how well they are supported by other sources, explaining why some may be biased

3.2 Evaluate the reasoning of an argument in a source, considering the structure and techniques used

My learning goals are to get better at:

- understanding the difference between audience and purpose in Global Perspectives
- explaining the difference between fact and opinion, and giving examples of each
- explaining bias in information sources

How will I know if I reach my goals?

As you work through this lesson, tick the 'Achieved' box to show you have achieved your learning goals. If you haven't quite achieved your learning goals, tick 'Not there yet'. Start to think about how you are going to show your learning goals in your challenge. Add an example from your challenge once you have achieved each learning goal.

Lesson 7	Not there yet	Achieved	Example
I understand the difference between audience and purpose in Global Perspectives.			
I can explain the difference between fact and opinion, and give examples of each.			
I can explain bias in an information source.			

Prior learning

1 What is the difference between the audience for an information source and the purpose of an information source? Discuss with a partner.

a Audience: ....

b Purpose: ....

2 Give an example for each:

a Audience: ....

b Purpose: ....

3 Share with another pair. Do the examples given show understanding of the terms 'audience' and purpose'? Write down better examples if necessary.

a Audience: ....

b Purpose: ....

Starter activity

1 Discuss the following questions with a partner and then write down your answers.

a What is a claim?

....

b Why do you need evidence to support a claim?

....

c What types of evidence can you use to support a claim?

....

d Why are counterarguments needed?

....

> **Tip**
> Bias is a judgement based on a personal point of view.

> **Tip**
> Reasoning is needed to justify a claim.

> **Tip**
> Bias can be seen as favouring a certain side.

> **Tip**
> A counter-argument opposes a claim or an argument. For example, 'Fairtrade is not fair' is a counterargument for 'Fairtrade is fair'.

Class discussion

2 Using what you've learnt from class discussion about claims, evidence and counterarguments, add further ideas in response to task 1. Add them in a different colour.

3 Using what you've learnt from class discussion about evidence, write down a definition for each of the terms 'fact' and 'opinion'.

a Fact: ....

b Opinion: ....

Peer feedback

4 Check your definitions with a partner. Do they have the same definitions as you? Make any changes in a different colour.

The topic I am working on today is ...

....

Main activity

1 Work with a partner. Using the topic/issue your teacher gives you, do some research to complete the following tasks:

a Write down one claim.

....

b Give reasoning for this claim.

....

c Give evidence to support this claim.

....

....

....

d Give a counterargument.

....

e Give an example of bias.

....

f Evaluate an individual piece of evidence.

....

....

2 Give your personal perspective about the topic/issue, giving reasons for this perspective.

....

....

> **Tip**
>
> An opinion can be used as evidence but is something that cannot be proven; it's what someone thinks, so it is weaker evidence than a fact.

> **Tip**
>
> A claim is a statement or assertion that something is a fact.

> **Tip**
>
> Evidence is needed to support a claim.

> **Tip**
>
> A fact can be used as evidence and is something that can be proven to be true.

> **Tip**
>
> A perspective is a certain view about or attitude towards a topic, sub-topic or issue.

Peer feedback

3 Give feedback to someone else in your class.

You understand . . .	Yes	Not yet	Action
what a claim is			
what reasoning is			
what evidence is			
what a counterargument is			
how to evaluate evidence			
how to give your personal perspective			

Tip

A personal perspective is your own view, supported by evidence and arrived at after the exploration of causes and consequences of an issue and the consideration of different perspectives.

Independent reflection activity

What skill did you improve today?

....

....

How did you improve it?

....

....

Check your learning

If you haven't already done so, complete the **How will I know if I reach my goals?** table with 'Not there yet' or 'Achieved'. Don't forget to add examples from your challenge.

Self-assessment 3

Look back at self-assessments 1 and 2. How much further progress do you feel you have made so far in developing your evaluation skills?

For each learning objective in the table below, shade in the response that matches yours most closely. Give one example for this response. Eventually, you are aiming for green!

Learning objectives: *to get better at understanding how to…*	RED	AMBER	GREEN
3.1 Evaluate a range of sources, considering the author and purpose and how well they are supported by other sources, explaining why some may be biased.	I can explain what evaluation is. I can recognise if information sources contain bias with help. I can identify the audience for and the purpose of different information sources with help.	I can explain what evaluation is. I can recognise if information sources contain bias. I can identify the audience for and the purpose of different information sources.	I can explain what evaluation is. I can recognise if information sources contain bias or are biased. I can explain the audience for and the purpose of different information sources. I can help others recognise bias in information sources and the audience for and purpose of different information sources.
3.2 Evaluate the reasoning of an argument in a source, considering the structure and techniques used.	I can evaluate the reasoning of an argument in an information source with help. I can recognise a claim, reasoning and evidence with help. I can recognise a counterargument with help. I know the difference between a fact and an opinion.	I can evaluate the reasoning of an argument in an information source. I can recognise a claim, reasoning and evidence. I can explain a counterargument. I can explain the difference between a fact and an opinion.	I can evaluate the reasoning of and argument in an information source. I can recognise claims, reasoning and evidence. I can explain counterarguments. I can help others recognise claims, reasoning, evidence and counterarguments in information sources. I can explain the difference between a fact and an opinion and give examples of both.

Continued

Examples:

3.1 ....

3.2 ....

Reflect on your responses in your self-assessment and identify two areas for improvement. Set yourself two learning targets – how you will improve upon the two areas. For example, 'I will ask my teacher to show me more examples of counterarguments so that I really understand what to look for in an information source.'

Learning targets:

1 Area for improvement: ....

How I will improve: ....

2 Area for improvement: ....

How I will improve: ....

Challenge topic review

Think about the challenge topic you have been exploring and complete the following statements.

I was surprised to discover that ....

....

I didn't know ....

....

I now think ....

....

> Section 4

Reflection

This section of your Learner's Skills Book 9 helps you to develop your reflection skills using interesting global topics.

Starting with . . .

As you start to develop reflection skills in Stage 9, you will be deepening your understanding of the difference between evaluation and reflection in Global Perspectives lessons. You will be identifying and explaining your personal strengths and abilities in relation to teamwork and identifying any areas for development. You will reflect on your personal contribution(s) to teamwork after working together towards a shared outcome and reflect on the challenges and benefits of teamwork. You will also start to explore your personal perspective on an issue and consider how this might have developed or changed.

Developing . . .

As you further develop your reflection skills in Stage 9, you will work as a team to plan and conduct research to gain information to produce questions for others to answer. You will develop your knowledge and understanding about your own contributions to teamwork in relation to your personal strengths and identify any areas that need improving to make teamwork more effective. You will also reflect on the skills you have learnt or improved during learning activities and consider how you might further develop these skills. You will think deeply about your personal perspective on an issue and how this has developed or changed as a result of the research conducted.

Getting better at . . .

As you get better at reflection in Stage 9, you will continue to focus on working as teams to discuss and plan courses of action that might help make a positive difference to an issue or resolve an issue. You will be participating in teamwork to develop your own personal strengths and identify any areas for improvement, and then you will consider strategies to develop your Global Perspectives skills. You will plan and produce a team outcome to achieve an aim and give and gain feedback on shared outcomes so you can make improvements. You will also explain how your personal perspective on an issue has changed or developed as a result of the research you have undertaken.

1

Starting with reflection skills: Lesson 1

4.1 Explain personal contribution to teamwork and relate to own strengths and areas for improvement

4.4 Identify skills learnt or improved during an activity and consider strategies for further development

My learning goals are to start to:

- explain the difference between evaluation and reflection in Global Perspectives
- explain personal strengths in relation to teamwork
- explain areas for development in relation to teamwork

How will I know if I reach my goals?

As you work through this lesson, tick the 'Achieved' box to show you have achieved your learning goals. If you haven't quite achieved your learning goals, tick 'Not there yet'. Start to think about how you are going to show your learning goals in your challenge. Add an example from your challenge once you have achieved each learning goal.

Lesson 1	Not there yet	Achieved	Example
I can explain the difference between evaluation and reflection in Global Perspectives.			
I can explain my personal strengths in relation to teamwork.			
I can explain areas for development in relation to teamwork.			

Prior learning

1 What do you think the term 'evaluation' means in Global Perspectives lessons?

Evaluation is ....

....

2 What do you think the term 'reflection' means in Global Perspectives lessons?

Reflection is ....

....

3 Do you agree with your classmates about the meanings of evaluation and reflection in Global Perspectives lessons? Yes/No

Why? ....

Make any changes to your definitions in task **1** if necessary.

Continued

4 Using what you have learnt from class discussion, explain the difference between evaluation and reflection in Global Perspectives lessons.

....

....

....

Starter activity

1 Which of these skills do you think you are good at? You may choose more than one.

- A Listening to the ideas of others ☐
- B Asking for help ☐
- C Helping others ☐
- D Asking questions ☐
- E Giving an opinion ☐
- F Researching for evidence ☐
- G Identifying claims ☐
- H Giving reasoning for claims ☐
- I Identifying counterarguments ☐
- J Summarising information in own words ☐
- K Other ....

2 Why do you think you have these strengths?

....

....

Tip

Reflective learners encourage feedback and respond positively to praise and criticism.

Tip

Reflective learners think about how they are learning when completing learning activities; for example, they might learn best by discussing with others or by doing research on their own.

Peer feedback

3 What does your partner think about your responses to task 1 and 2?

....

....

4 Which of the personal strengths identified in task 1 have you found useful in teamwork?

....

....

Why? ....

....

5 Which skills do you need to develop further?

....

Why?

....

Tip

Reflective learners can identify their personal strengths and explain these to others.

Tip

Reflective learners can identify any areas they need to develop, such as their listening or research skills.

The topic I am working on today is …

....

Tip

Reflective learners can explain how they are going to improve or develop a skill; for example, improving reflective skills by asking themselves regularly how they learn best and whether their perspective about something has changed or developed.

Main activity

1 In a small group, discuss the text your teacher gives you and then answer the following questions:

a What is the text about?

....

b What does each paragraph tell you?

Paragraph 1 (claim, reasoning, evidence):

....

....

....

Paragraph 2 (claim, reasoning, evidence):

....

....

....

Paragraph 3 (claim, reasoning, evidence):

....

....

....

Paragraph 4 (claim, reasoning, evidence):

....

....

....

2 Get into new groups. Share your information with your new group. Did sharing help you to understand better the claims, evidence and reasoning presented?

....

Why?

....

....

> **Tip**
>
> Sharing and discussing with others allows you to clarify your own thinking and learning, see things from different perspective and gain new ideas you might not have thought about before.

Class discussion

3 After class discussion about the whole text, do you now have a clearer understanding about the claims, reasoning for these claims and evidence to support these claims?

....

Why do you think this is?

....

Independent reflection activity

Which skill(s) did you use or improve this lesson?

....

....

How?

....

....

Which skill(s) do you need to develop further?

....

....

....

How are you going to improve the skill(s) you have identified?

....

....

Check your learning

If you haven't already done so, complete the **How will I know if I reach my goals?** table with 'Not there yet' or 'Achieved'. Don't forget to add examples from your challenge.

2

Starting with reflection skills: Lesson 2

4.1 Explain personal contribution to teamwork and relate to own strengths and areas for improvement

4.2 Relate benefits and challenges of teamwork to personal experience of working together to achieve a shared outcome and identify targets for improvement

My learning goals are to start to:

- explain personal contributions to teamwork
- explain the benefits and challenges of working as a team

How will I know if I reach my goals?

As you work through this lesson, tick the 'Achieved' box to show you have achieved your learning goals. If you haven't quite achieved your learning goals, tick 'Not there yet'. Start to think about how you are going to show your learning goals in your challenge. Add an example from your challenge once you have achieved each learning goal.

Lesson 2	Not there yet	Achieved	Example
I can explain my personal contribution(s) to teamwork.			
I can explain the benefits and challenges of working as a team.			

Prior learning

1 What do you think are the three most important abilities when working as a team? Discuss with a partner.

1 ....

2 ....

3 ....

2 Share with another pair. Do they agree? Make any changes if necessary.

1 ....

2 ....

3 ....

3 As a class, discuss the necessary abilities for working as a team. What ability do you think you need to focus on improving this lesson to make you a more effective team member?

....

Why?

....

Starter activity

1 Using what you've learnt from your Prior learning, what do you think the benefits and challenges of teamwork are and why? Work in pairs.

Benefits of teamwork ....

....

....

Challenges of teamwork ....

....

....

Tip

Effective teamwork relies on the combination of individual strengths and abilities brought to the team.

Peer feedback

2 Share your thinking with another pair. Do they have further ideas?

....

....

> **Tip**
>
> Working as a team is different to working in a team. To work as a team, you need to work with a group of people to achieve a shared goal or outcome in an effective way.

The topic I am working on today is …

....

Main activity

1 Look at the set of questions your teacher gives you. Discuss the questions and your answers with your team.

2 Produce a diagram on a separate sheet of paper, noting your team's responses to the questions. For example, you could use a mind map or a spider diagram.

3 Write down any other questions you could ask about the topic. Discuss them with your team, then add any further responses to your diagram.

....

....

....

....

....

....

> **Tip**
>
> It's important that each member of the team knows what they are doing to contribute to the team effort.

Independent reflection activity

What contribution(s) did you make to teamwork today?

....

....

What do you think were the challenges of working as a team in the Main activity?

....

....

Why? ....

....

What do you think were the benefits of working as a team in the Main activity today?

....

....

Why? ....

....

Check your learning

If you haven't already done so, complete the **How will I know if I reach my goals?** table with 'Not there yet' or 'Achieved'. Don't forget to add examples from your challenge.

3

Starting with reflection skills: Lesson 3

4.1 Explain personal contribution to teamwork and relate to own strengths and areas for improvement

4.2 Relate benefits and challenges of teamwork to personal experience of working together to achieve a shared outcome and identify targets for improvement

4.3 Explain how personal perspective on an issue has changed as a result of conducting research and exploring different perspectives

My learning goals are to start to:

- explain the benefits and challenges of teamwork
- explain my personal contribution(s) to teamwork
- explain area(s) for improvement in teamwork
- explore my personal perspective on a topic/an issue

How will I know if I reach my goals?

As you work through this lesson, tick the 'Achieved' box to show you have achieved your learning goals. If you haven't quite achieved your learning goals, tick 'Not there yet'. Start to think about how you are going to show your learning goals in your challenge. Add an example from your challenge once you have achieved each learning goal.

Lesson 3	Not there yet	Achieved	Example
I can explain the benefits and challenges of teamwork.			
I can explain my contribution(s) to teamwork.			
I can explain area(s) for improvement in teamwork.			
I can reflect on my personal perspective about a topic/an issue.			

Prior learning

1 Look back at your Prior learning from Lesson 2.

a Did you improve the ability you identified? Yes/No

b How did you improve this ability?

....

2 Discuss your responses to task 1 with your team. Write down all the abilities that were improved by your team members.

....

....

....

....

....

Tip

When reflecting on the benefits of teamwork, think about what you personally gain from working as a team.

Tip

When reflecting on the challenges of teamwork, think about what you and others might not like about working as a team.

The topic I am working on today is ...

....

Starter activity

For the Main activity in this lesson, your team will prepare and give a presentation to another team using your responses to the questions in the Main activity in Lesson 2.

Working in your team, look back at your diagram from Lesson 2 and consider the personal abilities and strengths in your team. Who will have the following responsibilities in preparing the presentation?

A Checking that everyone is listening to each other ....

B Making sure that everyone is working to the time limit ....

C Making sure that all ideas are appreciated ....

D Checking the clarity of the presentation, including spelling and grammar ....

E Making sure there is no conflict or that any conflict is resolved

....

F Encouraging the team to work together ....

G Searching for and suggesting suitable images ....

> **Tip**
>
> A personal strength or quality is something that you are good at.

> **Tip**
>
> A limitation or weakness is usually something that is lacking or not done very well.

> **Tip**
>
> An area for development is something you need to improve on.

Main activity

1 Using the information gained from the Main activity in Lesson 2 and the responsibilities from the Starter activity in this lesson, plan a team presentation. The purpose of your presentation is to explain your team's views about the topic in Lesson 2 to another team in your class.

As a team, you need to present five slides. The first slide will show the title of your topic. Each of the other four slides will show an image and about four bullet points. The fifth slide will be the conclusion. Plan each of your slides on a separate sheet of paper with:

- an image, or notes about it
- the bullet points for your slide
- notes to remind yourself what you want to say in the presentation.

Your plans for one slide might look like this:

Slide 2 ....

Image:

- ....
- ....
- ....
- ....

Notes ....

....

....

....

....

....

2 Give feedback on another team's presentation.
Answer the following questions.

a Did the presentation have a suitable title? Yes/No

b Was the content of the presentation clear? Yes/No

c Did the images used make the presentation more effective? Yes/No

d Was the content of the presentation interesting? Yes/No

e Was the presentation delivered in an enthusiastic way? Yes/No

f How might the presentation be improved?

....

....

Tip

A personal perspective is the view that a person has on a topic/an issue after exploring different perspectives and reflecting on the causes and consequences of an issue.

Independent reflection activity

What were the benefits of working as a team this lesson?

....

....

What were the challenges of working as a team this lesson?

....

....

What was your actual contribution to teamwork this lesson?
How did this help towards the shared goal/outcome?

....

....

What do you need to improve on for the next teamwork activity? Why?

....

....

What is your personal perspective on the topic studied this lesson?

....

....

....

Check your learning

If you haven't already done so, complete the **How will I know if I reach my goals?** table with 'Not there yet' or 'Achieved'. Don't forget to add examples from your challenge.

Self-assessment 1

How much progress do you feel you have made so far in developing your reflection skills?

For each learning objective in the table below, shade in the response that matches yours most closely. Give one example for this response. Eventually, you are aiming for green!

Learning objectives: *to start to …*	RED	AMBER	GREEN
4.1 Explain personal contribution to teamwork and relate to own strengths and areas for improvement.	I can explain my personal strengths in relation to teamwork with help. I can explain my contribution(s) to teamwork with help. I can explain at least one area for development in relation to teamwork with help.	I can explain my personal strengths in relation to teamwork. I can explain my contribution(s) to teamwork. I can explain at least one area for development in relation to teamwork.	I can explain my personal strengths in relation to teamwork. I can explain my contribution(s) to teamwork. I can explain at least one area for development in relation to teamwork. I can help others explain their personal strengths, areas for development and contribution(s) to teamwork.
4.2 Relate benefits and challenges of teamwork to personal experience of working together to achieve a shared outcome and identify targets for improvement.	I can explain some of the benefits and challenges of teamwork in relation to my personal experience with help.	I can explain some of the benefits and challenges of teamwork in relation to my personal experience.	I can explain the benefits and challenges of teamwork in relation to my personal experience and can help others explain the benefits and challenges of teamwork in relation to their personal experience.

Continued

Learning objectives: *to start to …*	RED	AMBER	GREEN
4.3 Explain how personal perspective on an issue has changed as a result of conducting research and exploring different perspectives.	I can explain how my personal perspective has developed/ changed as a result of conducting research and exploring different perspectives with help.	I can explain how my personal perspective has developed/ changed as a result of conducting research and exploring different perspectives.	I can explain how my personal perspective has developed/changed as a result of conducting research and exploring different perspectives. I can help others explain how their personal perspective has developed/changed as a result of conducting research and exploring different perspectives.
4.4 Identify skills learnt or improved during an activity and consider strategies for further development.	I can say what skills I have learnt or improved with help. I can say how I have learnt or improved a skill with help. I can say how I will improve a skill with help.	I can say what skills I have learnt or improved. I can say how I have learnt or improved a skill. I can say how I will improve a skill.	I can say what skills I have learnt or improved. I can say how I have learnt or improved a skill. I can say how I will improve a skill. I can help others say what skills they have learnt or improved and how they have done this and help them identify how to improve a skill in the future.

Examples:

4.1 ....

4.2 ....

4.3 ....

4.4 ....

Continued

Reflect on your responses in your self-assessment and identify two areas for improvement. Set yourself two learning targets – how you will improve upon the two areas. For example, 'I will try to appreciate all ideas, even though we might not use them all in our shared outcome'.

Learning targets:

1 Area for improvement: ....

How I will improve: ....

2 Area for improvement: ....

How I will improve: ....

Challenge topic review

Think about the challenge topic you have been exploring and complete the following statements.

I was surprised to discover that ....

....

I didn't know ....

....

I now think ....

....

4

Developing reflection skills: Lesson 4

4.1 Explain personal contribution to teamwork and relate to own strengths and areas for improvement

My learning goals are to develop my knowledge and understanding about:

- my contribution(s) to teamwork
- setting targets to improve my contribution(s) to teamwork

How will I know if I reach my goals?

As you work through this lesson, tick the 'Achieved' box to show you have achieved your learning goals. If you haven't quite achieved your learning goals, tick 'Not there yet'. Start to think about how you are going to show your learning goals in your challenge. Add an example from your challenge once you have achieved each learning goal.

Lesson 4	Not there yet	Achieved	Example
I can explain my contribution(s) to teamwork.			
I can set realistic targets to improve my contribution(s) to teamwork.			

Prior learning

1 Do you think working with others as a team presents more benefits or more challenges? Why?

I think ....

because ....

....

2 What does your partner think? Why?

My partner thinks ....

because ....

3 Using what you've learnt from class discussion about the benefits and challenges of teamwork, has your response to task 1 changed or not? Why?

....

....

4 How might you overcome any challenges?

....

The topic I am working on today is …

....

Starter activity

1 Working independently, write down all the words and phrases about the topic as you can in the time your teacher gives you.

Peer feedback

2 Add to your diagram in a different colour after discussion with your partner.

> **Tip**
>
> To overcome challenges in teamwork, you need to be prepared to listen to others and compromise if you don't totally agree with something.

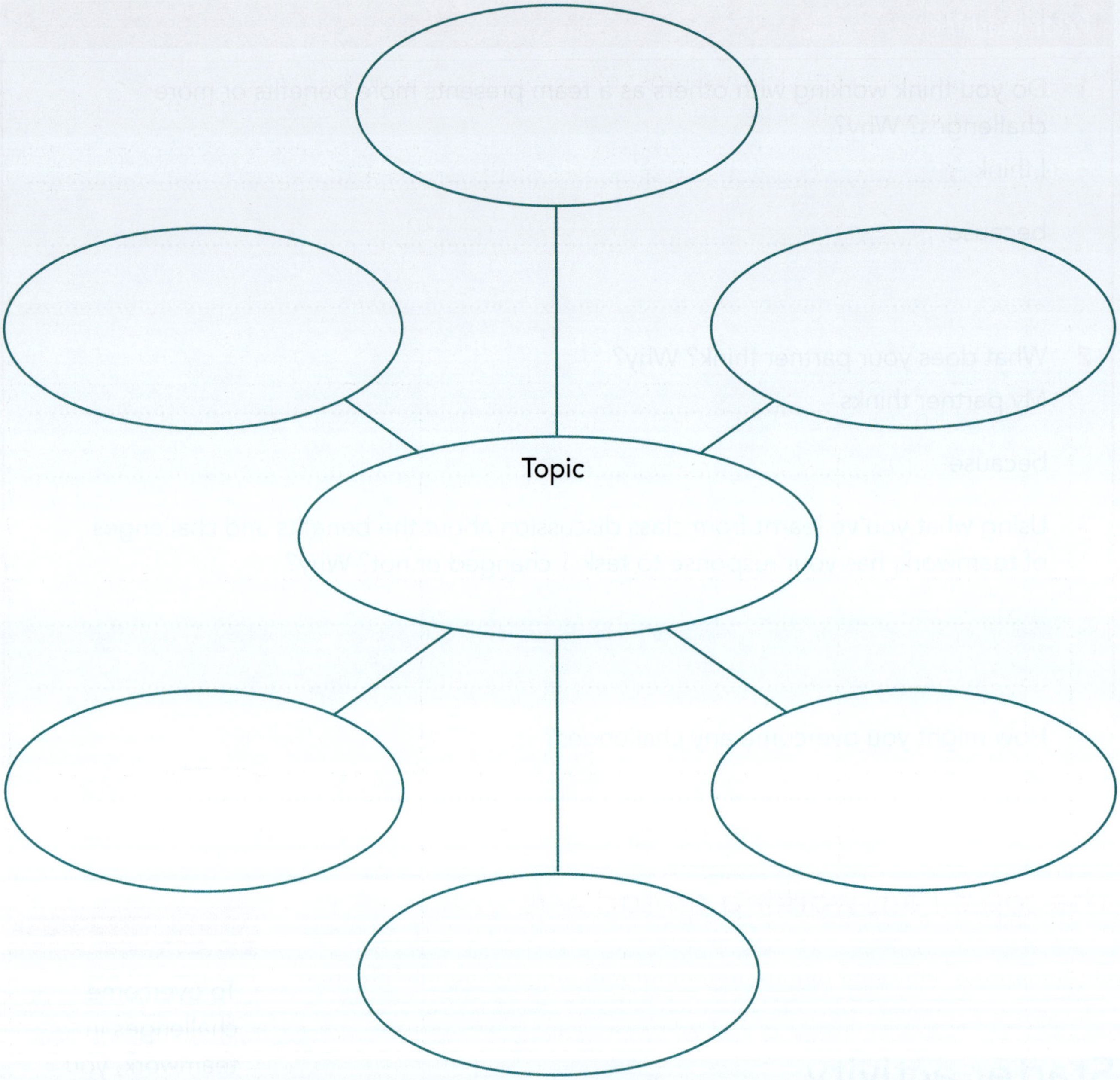

Class discussion

3 Add to your diagram in a different colour after class discussion.

Main activity

1 Decide what research each member of your team is going to do to find out more about the topic.

	Name	Research focus	Websites/Information sources
1			
2			
3			
4			
5			

2 Now that you have your research focus, complete the grid below.

a Make a brief note of different things you want to find out about. Then write one or two questions about each thing.

b Do some research and find an answer to each question.

My research is about:			
My information sources/website addresses:			
	What I want to find out about	Questions	Answers
1			
2			
3			
4			
5			
6			

Tips

Before starting your research, think about what you want to find out. This will make your search for information easier.

Tell someone else about what you've read. This will make sure you understand what you've read and that you can use your own words.

When making notes, ask yourself questions and put the answers from the information source into your own words.

Questions that start with 'what', 'when', 'where' and 'who' are good questions for finding out facts.

Questions that start with 'why' and 'how' help you gain details to develop your understanding about an issue or a perspective.

Independent reflection activity

What contributions(s) did you make to teamwork this lesson?

....

....

What personal strength(s) did you develop by contributing to teamwork this lesson?

....

....

What is/are your target(s) for improving your contribution(s) to teamwork next lesson?

....

....

Check your learning

If you haven't already done so, complete the **How will I know if I reach my goals?** table with 'Not there yet' or 'Achieved'. Don't forget to add examples from your challenge.

5

Developing reflection skills: Lesson 5

4.1 Explain personal contribution to teamwork and relate to own strengths and areas for improvement

4.4 Identify skills learnt or improved during an activity and consider strategies for further development

My learning goals are to develop my knowledge and understanding about:

- how contributing to teamwork develops personal strengths
- how reflection on skills learnt or improved helps to develop skills

How will I know if I reach my goals?

As you work through this lesson, tick the 'Achieved' box to show you have achieved your learning goals. If you haven't quite achieved your learning goals, tick 'Not there yet'. Start to think about how you are going to show your learning goals in your challenge. Add an example from your challenge once you have achieved each learning goal.

Lesson 5	Not there yet	Achieved	Example
I am increasing my contributions to teamwork.			
I am developing my personal strengths.			
I can explain how I have learnt or improved my skill(s).			
I can explain how to develop skills/a skill.			

Prior learning

With your team, consider your responses to the Independent reflection activity you did in Lesson 4.

1 What contribution(s) did you make to teamwork in Lesson 4?

....

....

2 What personal strength(s) did you develop by contributing to teamwork in Lesson 4?

....

....

3 What is/are your target(s) for improving your contribution(s) to teamwork this lesson?

....

....

4 Share your responses with your team. Do they agree that your target(s) will help improve teamwork? Yes/No

5 Make any changes to your target(s) after feedback if necessary.

....

....

The topic I am working on today is ...

....

Starter activity

1 Look at the questions you wrote for task **2** in the Main activity in Lesson 4.

Which do you think are your best three questions?

1 ....

2 ....

3 ....

2 Share your questions with a partner in your team.
As a pair, agree on the best three questions.

1 ....

2 ....

3 ....

3 Share your best three questions with your team.
As a team, decide on the best eight questions to ask another team to answer.
Try to include a variety of question starters (not just 'what . . . ?').

1 ....

2 ....

3 ....

4 ....

5 ....

6 ....

7 ....

8 ....

Main activity

1 a Working as a team, use this grid to record the questions another team has given you.

b Individually or in pairs, do some research to discover the answers.

c Then fill in the answers as a team.

Research topic: From team:		
	Questions	**Answers**
1		
2		
3		
4		
5		
6		
7		
8		

2 Record any further interesting information you find out about the topic.

....

....

....

....

Tip

Always take notes about any information that influences your own opinion about a topic. You will find this useful when reflecting on how your personal perspective has developed or changed.

Tip

When researching a topic, you will often come across interesting information that you can use to develop a perspective or to explain the causes and consequences of something, so don't forget to take notes.

Independent reflection activity

1 What skill have you used or improved today?

....

2 Do you think this skill is now becoming a personal strength? Yes/No

Why? ....

3 Did you improve your contributions(s) to teamwork this lesson? Yes/No

How? ....

Why not? ....

4 What skill(s) are you going to focus on improving next lesson so that more effective teamwork can take place?

....

5 How are you going to improve this/these skill(s)?

....

Check your learning

If you haven't already done so, complete the **How will I know if I reach my goals?** table with 'Not there yet' or 'Achieved'. Don't forget to add examples from your challenge.

6

Developing reflection skills: Lesson 6

4.2 Relate benefits and challenges of teamwork to personal experience of working together to achieve a shared outcome and identify targets for improvement

4.3 Explain how personal perspective on an issue has changed as a result of conducting research and exploring different perspectives

My learning goals are to develop my knowledge and understanding about:

- effective teamwork and how to overcome any challenges
- developing or changing a personal perspective using evidence from research and different perspectives

How will I know if I reach my goals?

As you work through this lesson, tick the 'Achieved' box to show you have achieved your learning goals. If you haven't quite achieved your learning goals, tick 'Not there yet'. Start to think about how you are going to show your learning goals in your challenge. Add an example from your challenge once you have achieved each learning goal.

Lesson 6	Not there yet	Achieved	Example
I can explain what effective teamwork is.			
I can explain how to overcome some of the challenges of teamwork.			
I can explain how my personal perspective about a topic has developed or changed using evidence from research and different perspectives.			

Prior learning

1 Why do you think conflict arises during teamwork?

....

....

2 Do your teammates agree with you?
Make any changes to your response to task 1 in a different colour.

3 How might you resolve any conflict during teamwork? Discuss the steps below within your team and put them in order, starting with the most important.

A Agree on the common goal for the team

B Request solutions to the problem/conflict

C Discuss ways to achieve the common goal

D Agree to get rid of any barriers to achieving the common goal

E Clarify what the problem is or what the conflict is about

F Agree on the best solution to the problem/conflict

G Discuss ways to achieve the common goal

Continued

H Stick to the agreed roles/responsibilities within the team

Most ....

....

....

....

....

....

....

Least ....

4 After class discussion about resolving conflict, make any changes to your responses for task **3** and add any further ways of resolving conflict you can think of.

Further ways of resolving conflict: ....

....

....

Starter activity

1 Consider your responses to the Independent reflection activity you did in Lesson 5. With your team, discuss the following questions.

a What skill are you going to focus on improving this lesson so that more effective teamwork can take place?

....

b How are you going to improve this skill?

....

Tip

Effective teamwork is only possible if any conflict is resolved quickly and if rules and responsibilities are agreed by all team members at the start.

2 Complete the table for each member of the team.

Name	**Skill** (e.g. communication; active listening; evaluation)	**Activity** (e.g. talk clearly; give verbal/non-verbal responses to suggestions; give peer feedback)

The topic I am working on today is ...

....

Main activity

1 On a separate sheet of paper, use the information you found out in the Main activity in Lesson 5 (in response to another teams' questions) to create a poster/infographic to present the information to your classmates.

2 As a team, give feedback to each of the other teams for their poster/infographic. Give each team two highlights and one area for improvement on a sticky note like the ones below.

Team:	Team:	Team:
Highlights:	Highlights:	Highlights:
Improvement:	Improvement:	Improvement:

Independent reflection activity

Reflect on your learning from viewing the posters/infographics in the Main activity. Answer the following questions.

Did you learn anything new this lesson? If so, what?

....

....

....

What did you think about the topic before you started working on it?

....

....

Has your personal perspective about the topic changed? Yes/No

How? ....

....

Why ....

....

Is your personal perspective about the topic the same but stronger? Yes/No

Why? ....

....

Tip

The ideas, experiences and perspectives of others all influence your own personal perspective.

You can change your personal perspective as a result of research and exploring different perspectives on a topic or issue.

Check your learning

If you haven't already done so, complete the **How will I know if I reach my goals?** table with 'Not there yet' or 'Achieved'. Don't forget to add examples from your challenge.

Self-assessment 2

Look back at self-assessment 1. How much further progress do you feel you have made so far in developing your reflection skills?

For each learning objective in the table below, shade in the response that matches yours most closely. Give one example for this response. Eventually, you are aiming for green!

Learning objectives: *to develop my knowledge and understanding about how to …*	RED	AMBER	GREEN
4.1 Explain personal contribution to teamwork and relate to own strengths and areas for improvement.	I can explain how I contribute to teamwork with help. I can explain how contributions to teamwork help develop my personal strengths with help. I can explain an area for improvement with help.	I can explain how I contribute to teamwork. I can explain how contributions to teamwork help develop my personal strengths. I can explain an area for improvement.	I can explain how I contribute to teamwork. I can explain how contributions to teamwork help develop my personal strengths. I can explain areas for improvement and help others identify areas for improvement for more effective teamwork.

Continued

Learning objectives: *to develop my knowledge and understanding about how to …*	RED	AMBER	GREEN
4.2 Relate benefits and challenges of teamwork to personal experience of working together to achieve a shared outcome and identify targets for improvement.	I can explain the benefits and challenges of teamwork in relation to my personal experience with help. I can describe some ways of overcoming challenges of teamwork with help.	I can explain the benefits and challenges of teamwork in relation to my personal experience. I can suggest some ways of overcoming some of the challenges of teamwork.	I can explain the benefits and challenges of teamwork in relation to my own and others' experiences and help others see the benefits and challenges of teamwork. I can explain ways of overcoming challenges in teamwork.
4.3 Explain how personal perspective on an issue has changed as a result of conducting research and exploring different perspectives.	I can give my personal perspective and support this with some evidence with help. I can explain how my personal perspective has developed/changed as a result of conducting research and exploring different perspectives with help.	I can give my personal perspective and support this with some evidence. I can explain how my personal perspective has developed/changed as a result of conducting research and exploring different perspectives with help.	I can give my personal perspective and support this with some evidence and help others use evidence to support their personal perspective. I can explain how my personal perspective has developed or changed as a result of conducting research and exploring different perspectives.
4.4 Identify skills learnt or improved during an activity and consider strategies for further development.	I can explain the skills I have learnt or improved with help. I can explain how I have learnt or improved a skill with help. I can explain how I will improve a skill with help.	I can explain the skills I have learnt or improved. I can explain how I have learnt or improved a skill. I can explain how I will improve a skill.	I can explain the skills I have learnt or improved. I can explain how I have learnt or improved a skill. I can explain how I will improve a skill. I can help others explain the skills they have learnt or improved and how they have learnt or improved them.

Continued

Examples:

4.1 ....

4.2 ....

4.3 ....

4.4 ....

Reflect on your responses in your self-assessment and identify two areas for improvement. Set yourself two learning targets – how you will improve upon the two areas. For example, 'I will check that I have referred to different perspectives when explaining how my personal perspective changed.'

Learning targets:

1 Area for improvement: ....

How I will improve: ....

2 Area for improvement: ....

How I will improve: ....

Challenge topic review

Think about the challenge topic you have been exploring and complete the following statements.

I was surprised to discover that ....

....

I didn't know ....

....

I now think ....

....

7

Getting better at reflection skills: Lesson 7

4.1 Explain personal contribution to teamwork and relate to own strengths and areas for improvement

4.4 Identify skills learnt or improved during an activity and consider strategies for further development

My learning goals are to get better at:

- participating in teamwork to develop personal strengths
- identifying areas for improvement during teamwork
- considering strategies to develop skills

How will I know if I reach my goals?

As you work through this lesson, tick the 'Achieved' box to show you have achieved your learning goals. If you haven't quite achieved your learning goals, tick 'Not there yet'. Start to think about how you are going to show your learning goals in your challenge. Add an example from your challenge once you have achieved each learning goal.

Lesson 7	Not there yet	Achieved	Example
I understand that I can develop my personal strengths by participating in teamwork.			
I can identify areas for improvement during teamwork.			
I know how to develop a skill.			

Prior learning

1 Which of these do you think are your personal strengths? You may choose more than one, but in task 2 you must give an example for each strength chosen.

	Personal strengths	Yes	No
A	I can do effective research		
B	I know what a shared outcome is		
C	I know the difference between a cause and a consequence		
D	I can determine the reliability of an information source		
E	I can support my personal perspective with evidence		
F	I am good at problem-solving		
G	I am an active listener		
H	I am able to share my ideas and opinions		
I	I am a good communicator		
J	I can compare a global perspective and a national perspective		
K	I can formulate a focused research question		
L	I can evaluate an information source in terms of its bias		
M	I am good at reflecting		

2 Which of the personal strengths you ticked 'yes' to have been developed through participating in teamwork?

....

....

3 After class discussion about personal strengths and teamwork, answer the following question.

Why do you think participating in teamwork helps develop personal strengths?

....

....

4 Share your ideas with your partner. Make any changes to your response to task 3 in a different colour.

The topic I am working on today is …

....

Starter activity

1 Look at the picture your teacher shows you. What is the issue in the picture?

....

2 What do you know about the issue?

....

....

....

3 What do you need to consider before suggesting a course of action to try to help resolve the issue?

....

....

....

Main activity

1 Work in teams. Consider the issue from the Starter activity and write it as a question.

....

Tip

It's always a good idea for each team member to do some of the research as well as having another role in producing the shared outcome.

Tip

When thinking about courses of action, consider how they will work to help resolve the issue or make a positive difference to an issue.

Tip

Try not to think too big. Think of a course of action you and your classmates can take such as creating a presentation or a series of posters to raise awareness about an issue to make people think differently.

2 Complete the table to decide on three possible courses of action.

Issue (as a question):		
Possible course of action	**Reasons for/against**	**Other** (e.g. questions to ask such as 'Who to involve?' 'How time consuming?' 'What resources are needed?')
1		
2		
3		

Class discussion

3 As a result of class discussion about possible courses of action, choose your team's best course of action from task 2. Explain why you have chosen this course of action.

Best course of action:

....

Reason:

....

....

Tip

The best course of action will allow you to meet your aim in a practical and achievable way. For example, if your aim is to raise awareness about equality of access to clean water, you might produce a series of posters showing people walking miles to collect water, droughts in certain areas, and images and text to encourage people to save or use less water or to give money to charities focused on achieving equality of access to clean water for all.

Independent reflection activity

What skill(s) have you learnt or improved today?

....

....

How have you done this? ....

....

What skill do you still need to improve?

....

....

Why do you still need to improve this skill? ....

....

....

How are you going to improve this skill?

....

....

Check your learning

If you haven't already done so, complete the **How will I know if I reach my goals?** table with 'Not there yet' or 'Achieved'. Don't forget to add examples from your challenge.

8

Getting better at reflection skills: Lesson 8

4.1 Explain personal contribution to teamwork and relate to own strengths and areas for improvement

4.4 Identify skills learnt or improved during an activity and consider strategies for further development

My learning goals are to get better at:

- explaining my personal contribution(s) to teamwork
- relating my contribution(s) to teamwork to my personal strengths and areas for improvement
- explaining skills learnt or improved

How will I know if I reach my goals?

As you work through this lesson, tick the 'Achieved' box to show you have achieved your learning goals. If you haven't quite achieved your learning goals, tick 'Not there yet'. Start to think about how you are going to show your learning goals in your challenge. Add an example from your challenge once you have achieved each learning goal.

Lesson 8	Not there yet	Achieved	Example
I can explain my personal contribution(s) to teamwork.			
I can relate my contribution(s) to teamwork to my personal strengths and areas for improvement.			
I can explain the skills that I have learnt or improved.			

Prior learning

1 In teams, review and discuss what the term 'course of action' means in Global Perspectives.

....

2 What do you need to consider when suggesting a course of action for an issue in Global Perspectives?

- ....
- ....
- ....

Starter activity

1 Look at the course of action you decided on in Lesson 7. Answer the questions.

a Is the course of action specific to the issue? Yes/No

because ....

Tip

A question to test if a course of action is measurable is 'How will we know if it's successful?'

b Is it measurable? Yes/No
because ....

c Is it achievable? Yes/No
because ....

d Is it realistic? Yes/No
because ....

e Can you do it in the time allowed? Yes/No
because ....

2 If you answered 'No' to any of the questions in task 1, you might need to change your course of action before planning and producing the first draft of your team outcome in the Main activity.

3 What is your team outcome?

....

Tips

A question to test if a course of action is realistic is 'Is it practical?'

A question to test if a course of action is time-bound (can be done in the time available) is 'Do we have enough time?'

Tip

Questions to test if a course of action is specific include 'Does it relate to the issue?' and 'What exactly are we trying to achieve?'

Tip

A question to test if a course of action is achievable is 'Can we do it within the given time?'

Tip

When planning, each member of a team needs a specific job as well as taking part in the research.

Tip

When planning, each member of a team needs a specific job as well as taking part in the research.

Main activity

1 Use this grid to record your team action plan for creating your team outcome.

<table>
<tr><td>Issue</td><td colspan="4"></td></tr>
<tr><td>Course of action</td><td colspan="4"></td></tr>
<tr><td>Team outcome</td><td colspan="4"></td></tr>
<tr><td>Team members</td><td colspan="4"></td></tr>
<tr><td>Start date</td><td>End date</td><td>Task (What?)
Action (How?)</td><td>Person to do it</td><td>Resources needed</td></tr>
<tr><td></td><td></td><td></td><td></td><td></td></tr>
<tr><td></td><td></td><td></td><td></td><td></td></tr>
<tr><td></td><td></td><td></td><td></td><td></td></tr>
<tr><td></td><td></td><td></td><td></td><td></td></tr>
<tr><td></td><td></td><td></td><td></td><td></td></tr>
</table>

2 Complete your draft team outcome on a separate sheet of paper.

Tips

Local research will involve talking with people who are experts in their field such as community leaders, teachers in school or parents who work for a specific company.

Identify the personal strengths of team members. Then allocate tasks according to these personal strengths.

Taking time at the beginning of a team project to allocate roles and responsibilities to team members according to their personal strengths is time well spent and will support more effective teamwork.

Peer feedback

3 Give and receive feedback on the team outcomes. What did your peers say about your team outcome? Answer the questions.

a Is the team outcome related to the issue? Yes/No

b Can it help towards resolving the issue? Yes/No

c Can it make a positive difference to the issue? Yes/No

d Are the key messages clear? Yes/No

e Does the team outcome include different perspectives? Yes/No

f Is it a realistic course of action? Yes/No

g Any other feedback?

....

....

....

Independent reflection activity

How did you contribute to teamwork today?

....

....

....

Continued

Which personal strength(s) did you improve by contributing to teamwork?

....

....

....

Which personal strength(s) still need(s) developing for you to become a more effective team member?

....

....

What skill did you learn or improve today?

....

....

What skill do you still need to improve?

....

....

How are you going to improve it?

....

....

Check your learning

If you haven't already done so, complete the **How will I know if I reach my goals?** table with 'Not there yet' or 'Achieved'. Don't forget to add examples from your challenge.

9

Getting better at reflection skills: Lesson 9

4.2 Relate benefits and challenges of teamwork to personal experience of working together to achieve a shared outcome and identify targets for improvement

4.3 Explain how personal perspective on an issue has changed as a result of conducting research and exploring different perspectives

My learning goals are to get better at:

- explaining the benefits and challenges of teamwork
- explaining how to overcome the challenges of teamwork
- explaining my personal perspective on an issue

How will I know if I reach my goals?

As you work through this lesson, tick the 'Achieved' box to show you have achieved your learning goals. If you haven't quite achieved your learning goals, tick 'Not there yet'. Start to think about how you are going to show your learning goals in your challenge. Add an example from your challenge once you have achieved each learning goal.

Lesson 9	Not there yet	Achieved	Example
I can explain some of the benefits and challenges of teamwork.			
I can explain how to overcome some of the challenges of teamwork.			
I can explain my personal perspective.			

Prior learning

In teams, discuss the benefits and challenges of teamwork.

1 What have been the benefits of teamwork so far?

....

....

2 Choose one challenge your team faced in Lesson 8.

....

3 What did you do to overcome this challenge?

....

....

4 How else might you overcome this challenge?

....

....

The topic I am working on today is …

....

> **Tip**
>
> When evaluating an outcome, as well as considering the limitations and areas for improvement, you also reflect on the highlights – the things the outcome does well.

Starter activity

Discuss the following questions with your team.

1 What feedback was given in Lesson 8 about your team outcome?

- ....
- ....
- ....

2 What changes do you need to make to improve your team outcome?

....

....

> **Tip**
>
> As well as asking your peers to evaluate your team outcome, ask the audience for whom you created the team outcome. Then you know if you have achieved what you set out to achieve.

Main activity

1 Complete your team outcome, making the changes you have identified.

2 Use this grid to evaluate your team outcome from the point of view of the target audience.

	Evaluating team outcome	Yes	No	Action
1	Is the outcome related to the issue?			
2	Do you think the outcome can help towards resolving the issue?			

	Evaluating team outcome	Yes	No	Action
3	Do you think the outcome can make a positive difference to the issue?			
4	Do you understand the key messages in the outcome?			
5	Does the outcome include different perspectives?			
6	Is the outcome a realistic course of action?			
7	Other evaluation questions?			

Tips

Work in your team to evaluate your team outcome as different members of the team will think different things.

Always try to give a reason and evidence to support your personal perspective. Say: 'I think this, because . . .'.

Independent reflection activity

1 Complete the following statements.

Before completing this section on reflection skills, I thought reflection was ....

....

....

Now, I think ....

....

....

This is due to ....

....

....

2 How has your personal perspective about the issue explored in Lessons 7–9 developed or changed?

....

....

....

3 Which evidence supports your personal perspective in task 2?

....

....

....

Check your learning

If you haven't already done so, complete the **How will I know if I reach my goals?** table with 'Not there yet' or 'Achieved'. Don't forget to add examples from your challenge.

Self-assessment 3

Look back at self-assessments 1 and 2. How much further progress do you feel you have made so far in developing your reflection skills?

For each learning objective in the table below, shade in the response that matches yours most closely. Give one example for this response. Eventually, you are aiming for green!

Learning objectives: *to get better at understanding how to …*	RED	AMBER	GREEN
4.1 Explain personal contribution to teamwork and relate to own strengths and areas for improvement.	I can explain how my contribution(s) to teamwork have helped to develop my personal strengths with help. I can explain how my contribution(s) to teamwork have helped me identify areas for improvement with help.	I can explain how my contribution(s) to teamwork have helped to develop my personal strengths. I can explain how my contribution(s) to teamwork have helped me identify areas for improvement.	I can explain how my contribution(s) to teamwork have helped to develop my personal strengths. I can explain how my contribution(s) to teamwork have helped me identify areas for improvement. I can help others explain how their contribution(s) to teamwork have helped to develop their personal strengths.
4.2 Relate benefits and challenges of teamwork to personal experience of working together to achieve a shared outcome and identify targets for improvement.	I can explain the benefits and challenges of teamwork in relation to my personal experiences with help. I can suggest some ways of overcoming challenges of teamwork with help.	I can explain the benefits and challenges of teamwork in relation to my personal experiences. I can explain how to overcome some of the challenges of teamwork.	I can explain the benefits and challenges of teamwork in relation to my own and others' experiences. I can explain ways of overcoming challenges in teamwork and help others suggest how to overcome some of the challenges of teamwork.

Continued

Learning objectives: *to get better at understanding how to …*	RED	AMBER	GREEN
4.3 Explain how personal perspective on an issue has changed as a result of conducting research and exploring different perspectives.	I understand what a personal perspective is. I can say if my personal perspective has developed or changed after research, and support this with some relevant evidence with help.	I understand what a personal perspective is. I can explain if my personal perspective has developed or changed after research, and support this with some relevant evidence.	I understand what a personal perspective is. I can explain if my personal perspective has developed or changed after research, and support this with relevant evidence. I can help others explain how their personal perspective on an issue has developed or changed after research and help them identify evidence to support their personal perspective.
4.4 Identify skills learnt or improved during an activity and consider strategies for further development.	I can explain why and how I have learnt or improved a skill with help. I can explain why and how I will further develop a skill with help.	I can explain why and how I have learnt or improved a skill. I can explain why and how I will further develop a skill.	I can explain why and how I have learnt or improved a skill and help others explain the importance of learning and improving skills. I can explain why and how I will further develop a skill and help others consider strategies for developing skills/a skill.

Continued

Examples:

4.1 ....

4.2 ....

4.3 ....

4.4 ....

Reflect on your responses in your self-assessment and identify two areas for improvement. Set yourself two learning targets – how you will improve upon the two areas. For example, 'I will try to explain a skill I have learnt and ask my teacher why this skill is important.'

Learning targets:

1 Area for improvement: ....

How I will improve: ....

2 Area for improvement: ....

How I will improve: ....

Challenge topic review

Think about the challenge topic you have been exploring and complete the following statements.

I was surprised to discover that ....

....

I didn't know ....

....

I now think ....

....

Section 5

Communication

This section of your Learner's Skills Book 9 helps you to develop your communication skills using interesting global topics.

Starting with . . .

As you start to develop your communication skills in Stage 9, you will be learning to explain the difference between a coherent and an incoherent text, and how a text is structured to enhance communication. You will also start to consider offering well-judged contributions to enhance your understanding of issues in Global Perspectives. You will focus on the features that help to make a coherent and clearly structured argument so that you can start to create your own well-reasoned arguments using claims, reasoning and supporting evidence. You will also start to give and receive feedback to improve work.

Developing . . .

As you further develop your communication skills in Stage 9, you will develop your knowledge and understanding about the importance of feedback – giving it and receiving it. You will be listening to and recording ideas and information to enhance your understanding of an issue and you will be developing your ability to present ideas and information clearly and with reasoning. You will continue to work independently, in pairs and in teams to explore interesting texts about global issues to enhance your understanding of Global Perspectives.

Getting better at . . .

As you get better at communicating with others in Stage 9, you will be exploring how to synthesise all the information and ideas gained about a global issue – its causes and consequences, different perspectives (global, national and personal) and courses of action. You will work creatively in teams to produce a shared outcome to raise awareness about a global issue of your choice.

1

Starting with communication skills: Lesson 1

5.1 Present coherent, well-reasoned and clearly structured arguments with detailed referencing of sources where appropriate

5.2 Listen to ideas and information and offer well-judged contributions that shape the discussion and enhance understanding of the issue

My learning goals are to start to:

- know the difference between a coherent and an incoherent text
- explain how a text is structured to enhance communication
- offer well-judged contributions to enhance my understanding of an issue

How will I know if I reach my goals?

As you work through this lesson, tick the 'Achieved' box to show you have achieved your learning goals. If you haven't quite achieved your learning goals, tick 'Not there yet'. Start to think about how you are going to show your learning goals in your challenge. Add an example from your challenge once you have achieved each learning goal.

Lesson 1	Not there yet	Achieved	Example
I know the difference between a coherent and an incoherent text.			
I can explain how a text is structured to enhance communication.			
I can offer well-judged contributions to enhance my understanding of an issue.			

Prior learning

1 Discuss with a partner. What do you think it means when text is coherent?

....

....

2 Discuss with a partner. What do you think it means when a text is incoherent?

....

....

3 Discuss with your classmates. Add further ideas in a different colour.

Starter activity

Look at the text your teacher shows you. Discuss it with a partner.

1 Do you think the text is coherent? Yes/No

Why?

....

....

Class discussion

2 Do your classmates agree?
Change or add to your ideas in a different colour.

....

The topic I am working on today is ...

....

Main activity

1 When thinking about the structure of any text, which of these features do you think is important? Discuss the list with a partner. Agree on the three most important features.

A The text contains understandable words and phrases
B There is an introduction
C The introduction introduces the main message
D The conclusion draws together the points made
E There are paragraphs
F Each point follows on from the next
G There is a heading/title
H Words and phrases are spelt correctly
I There is a reference list

1 ....

2 ....

3 ....

> **Tip**
>
> Text structure is about how the text is organised so that the reader can follow it easily.

> **Tip**
>
> For Global Perspectives, a paragraph will present a claim, reasoning to justify the claim and evidence to support the claim.

2 Explain why you have chosen these features.

1 ....

2 ....

3 ....

Class discussion

3 Using what you have learnt from class discussion, why do you think it's important that texts have structure?

....

....

4 Look at the text your teacher shows you.

a What is the main message in the text?

....

b How many paragraphs are there? What is the key idea in each paragraph?

....

....

....

c Do the ideas in each paragraph follow on from each other? Give an example.

....

....

d Is there a conclusion? If so, does the conclusion sum up the points made in the rest of the text?

....

e Is there a heading/title? Does this relate to the content of the text?

....

f Is there a reference list? If so, is it accurate?

....

g Do you understand all the words and phrases? Are they spelt correctly?

....

> **Tip**
>
> If a text is coherent, it makes sense through the organisation of its content. In writing, coherence is provided by a clear and understood structuring of paragraphs and sentences.

> **Tip**
>
> The opposite of coherence is incoherence. If a text is incoherent, it generally doesn't make sense and is difficult to read and follow.

h Do you think this text is well-structured? Yes/No

Why? ....

Peer feedback

5 Discuss your responses with your group. Using what you have learnt from class discussion, add any further ideas to your responses to **a–h** in a different colour.

Tip

Global Perspectives texts are usually made up of 1) an introduction linked to the heading/title/research question, 2) main points: claims, reasoning and evidence and 3) a conclusion summing up the evidence and reflecting on personal perspective.

Tip

In Global Perspectives, a conclusion is important to reflect on your own personal perspective about the issue after exploring the causes, consequences and different perspectives.

Independent reflection activity

Did sharing your ideas with your partner and classmates help your understanding of the following:

a Coherence Yes/No

b Incoherence Yes/No

c Text structure Yes/No

What skill(s) did you use today?

....

....

How?

....

....

Check your learning

If you haven't already done so, complete the **How will I know if I reach my goals?** table with 'Not there yet' or 'Achieved'. Don't forget to add examples from your challenge.

2

Starting with communication skills: Lesson 2

5.1 Present coherent, well-reasoned and clearly structured arguments with detailed referencing of sources where appropriate

5.2 Listen to ideas and information and offer well-judged contributions that shape the discussion and enhance understanding of the issue

My learning goals are to start to:

- explain the features that help to make a coherent and clearly structured argument in Global Perspectives
- create a well-reasoned argument with a claim, reasoning and supporting evidence
- offer well-judged contributions to enhance understanding of an issue

How will I know if I reach my goals?

As you work through this lesson, tick the 'Achieved' box to show you have achieved your learning goals. If you haven't quite achieved your learning goals, tick 'Not there yet'. Start to think about how you are going to show your learning goals in your challenge. Add an example from your challenge once you have achieved each learning goal.

Lesson 2	Not there yet	Achieved	Example
I can explain the features that help to make a coherent and clearly structured argument in Global Perspectives.			
I can create a well-reasoned argument with a claim, reasoning and supporting evidence.			
I can offer well-judged contributions to enhance understanding of an issue.			

Prior learning

1 Which of these features helps to make a coherent and clearly structured argument in Global Perspectives?

	Features	Yes (✓)
1	conclusion	
2	different perspectives	
3	paragraphs	
4	punctuation	
5	claims	
6	makes sense	
7	introduction	
8	reasoning	
9	reference list	
10	title/heading	
11	grammatically correct	

Continued

	Features	Yes (✓)
12	supporting evidence	
13	relevant words and phrases	
14	sub-headings	
15	transition words	

2 Discuss the features with your partner. Which ones do you and your partner agree on?

....

3 Why do you think these features are important?

....

....

The topic I am working on today is ...

....

Starter activity

1 Look at the sub-topic your teacher gives you. Discuss it with a partner. Write down three claims that might be appropriate to the sub-topic.

1 ....

2 ....

3 ....

2 Find another pair with the same sub-topic. Discuss all the claims. Choose one claim to create an argument in the Main activity.

....

Tip

A claim is an assertion that something is true.

Main activity

Use your chosen claim from the Starter activity. As a group, research ideas for an argument for your claim and record your ideas in this table.

Claim:	
Introduction	
Middle paragraphs	
Conclusion	

Tip

The introduction should make it clear what the argument is about and link to your claim.

Tip

The middle will be made up of more than one paragraph. Each paragraph will include a claim, justification for this claim and evidence to support each claim made.

Tip

The conclusion should not bring in any new ideas. It should only sum up the main existing ideas, briefly summarising any supporting evidence. In Global Perspectives, the conclusion will also contain your personal perspective linked to your research and evidence.

Independent reflection activity

How did you learn best today?

....

....

How did you help someone else learn today?

....

....

What skill(s) did you use or improve today? How?

....

....

....

Check your learning

If you haven't already done so, complete the **How will I know if I reach my goals?** table with 'Not there yet' or 'Achieved'. Don't forget to add examples from your challenge.

3

Starting with communication skills: Lesson 3

5.1 Present coherent, well-reasoned and clearly structured arguments with detailed referencing of sources where appropriate

5.2 Listen to ideas and information and offer well-judged contributions that shape the discussion and enhance understanding of the issue

My learning goals are to start to:

- explain the features that help to create a coherent and clearly structured argument in Global Perspectives
- create a coherent and clearly structured argument with claims/a claim, reasoning and supporting evidence
- give and receive feedback to improve an argument

How will I know if I reach my goals?

As you work through this lesson, tick the 'Achieved' box to show you have achieved your learning goals. If you haven't quite achieved your learning goals, tick 'Not there yet'. Start to think about how you are going to show your learning goals in your challenge. Add an example from your challenge once you have achieved each learning goal.

Lesson 3	Not there yet	Achieved	Example
I can explain some of the features that help to create a coherent and clearly structured argument in Global Perspectives.			
I can create a well-reasoned argument, with claims/a claim, reasoning and supporting evidence.			
I can give and receive feedback to improve work.			

Prior learning

1 What features help create a coherent and clearly structured argument in Global Perspectives?

1 ....

2 ....

3 ....

2 Using what you've learnt from class discussion, add two further features.

4 ....

5 ....

The topic I am working on today is …

....

Starter activity

1 Review the notes for your argument from the Main activity in Lesson 2.

2 Add any further ideas.

Main activity

1 Write the script for your argument. You might also do this on a separate sheet of paper.

Claim:	
Introduction	
Middle paragraphs	
Conclusion	

Tip

You should start a new paragraph when you begin a new idea or point; to compare information; and when you are ending your introduction or starting your conclusion.

Tip

When writing the conclusion of an argument, use transition words such as 'Finally', 'In conclusion', 'To sum up', 'As you can see'.

Tip

When presenting reasoning for claims/a claim, use transition words such as 'because', 'due to', 'additionally'.

Tip

When referring to evidence in an argument, use transition words such as 'for example', 'for instance', 'to demonstrate'.

Peer feedback

2 As a team, discuss your script and make any amendments necessary.

3 Check your script by completing this table.

Claim:			
Title:			
Is/are there . . .	**Yes**	**No**	**Notes**
an introduction (including title)			
a conclusion (including personal perspective)			
a middle with claims			
reasoning to justify the claims in the middle			
supporting evidence for the claims in the middle			
a reference list			
transition words/phrases (e.g. therefore, so, in summary)			
accurate spelling			
relevant topic-specific words and phrases			
punctuation			
paragraphs			
different perspectives			
a logical structure			
correct grammatical structures			

Tip

When giving feedback, always start with the positive; for example, 'It's good to see . . .'

Tip

Be prepared to give an example for any points you make that will help improve someone else's work.

Tip

When giving feedback, always give more positives than negatives; for example, two highlights and one area for improvement.

Tip

Remember that good feedback is not personal; it's about the work produced.

4 Give feedback to another team on their script using the table in task 3.

Independent reflection activity

Which skill did you improve this lesson?

....

....

How did you improve it?

....

....

Which skill do you still need to work on?

....

....

How are you going to do this?

....

....

Check your learning

If you haven't already done so, complete the **How will I know if I reach my goals?** table with 'Not there yet' or 'Achieved'. Don't forget to add examples from your challenge.

Self-assessment 1

How much progress do you feel you have made so far in developing your communication skills?

For each learning objective in the table below, shade in the response that matches yours most closely. Give one example for this response. Eventually, you are aiming for green!

Learning objectives: *to start to …*	RED	AMBER	GREEN
5.1 Present coherent, well-reasoned and clearly structured arguments with detailed referencing of sources where appropriate.	I can identify a coherent and clearly structured text with help. I can identify a claim, reasoning and evidence with help. I can write a paragraph including a claim, reasoning and evidence with help.	I can identify a coherent and clearly structured text. I can identify a claim, reasoning and evidence. I can write a paragraph including a claim, reasoning and evidence.	I can identify a coherent and clearly structured text and help others to identify coherent and clearly structured texts. I can identify a claim, reasoning and evidence. I can write a paragraph including a claim, reasoning and evidence.
5.2 Listen to ideas and information and offer well-judged contributions that shape the discussion and enhance understanding of the issue.	I can listen to ideas and information, and note the main points with help. I can offer some contributions to discussions with help, although they may not always be relevant or well-judged.	I can listen to ideas and information, and note the main points. I can offer some relevant contributions to discussions to help enhance my own understanding of an issue.	I can listen to ideas and information, and note the main points. I can help others note the main points from discussions. I can offer relevant contributions to discussions to help enhance my own understanding of an issue, and help others understand the issue.

Examples:

5.1 ....

5.2 ....

Continued

Reflect on your responses in your self-assessment and identify two areas for improvement. Set yourself two learning targets – how you will improve upon the two areas. For example, 'I can help others understand the issue by offering more ideas in discussions.'

Learning targets:

1 Area for improvement: ....

How I will improve: ....

2 Area for improvement: ....

How I will improve: ....

Challenge topic review

Think about the challenge topic you have been exploring and complete the following statements.

I was surprised to discover that ....

....

I didn't know ....

....

I now think ....

....

Developing communication skills: Lesson 4

5.1 Present coherent, well-reasoned and clearly structured arguments with detailed referencing of sources where appropriate

5.2 Listen to ideas and information and offer well-judged contributions that shape the discussion and enhance understanding of the issue

My learning goals are to develop my knowledge and understanding about:

- the importance of feedback
- listening to and recording ideas and information to enhance understanding of an issue

How will I know if I reach my goals?

As you work through this lesson, tick the 'Achieved' box to show you have achieved your learning goals. If you haven't quite achieved your learning goals, tick 'Not there yet'. Start to think about how you are going to show your learning goals in your challenge. Add an example from your challenge once you have achieved each learning goal.

Lesson 4	Not there yet	Achieved	Example
I understand the importance of giving and receiving feedback.			
I can listen to and record relevant ideas and information to enhance my understanding of an issue.			

Prior learning

Discuss the following questions with your team.

1 Why is feedback important?

....

2 What do you need to remember when giving feedback?

....

....

3 Does your partner agree? Add any further ideas in a different colour.

....

Starter activity

1 Discuss the feedback given to your team on your argument in Lesson 3.

2 As a team, improve your script using the feedback.

Claim:	
Introduction	
Middle paragraphs	
Conclusion	

3 Record your argument as a podcast or get ready to read it aloud to another team.

Main activity

1 Listen to another team's argument. As you listen, make your own independent notes to complete the table.

Claim:			
Title:			
Is/are there . . .	Yes	No	Notes
an introduction (including title)			
a conclusion (including personal perspective)			
a middle with claims			
reasoning to justify the claims in the middle			
supporting evidence for the claims in the middle			

Is/are there . . .	Yes	No	Notes
transition words/phrases (e.g. therefore, so, in summary)			
relevant topic-specific words and phrases			
different perspectives			
a logical structure			

2 Share your notes from task **1** with your team.
Give overall feedback to the other team on their argument.

Claim:	
Title:	
Team:	

Independent reflection activity

Do you think listening to the ideas of others helped with your own understanding of the issue? Yes/No

Why? ....

....

Which part of today's lesson helped you learn most?

....

....

Why?

....

....

On a scale of 1–10, with 10 being the most, what effort did you put into today's lesson? Give a reason why you have scored yourself this number.

My effort in today's lesson									
1	**2**	**3**	**4**	**5**	**6**	**7**	**8**	**9**	**10**

Reason(s): ....

....

....

Check your learning

If you haven't already done so, complete the **How will I know if I reach my goals?** table with 'Not there yet' or 'Achieved'. Don't forget to add examples from your challenge.

5

Developing communication skills: Lesson 5

5.1 Present coherent, well-reasoned and clearly structured arguments with detailed referencing of sources where appropriate

5.2 Listen to ideas and information and offer well-judged contributions that shape the discussion and enhance understanding of the issue

My learning goals are to develop my knowledge and understanding about:

- presenting ideas and information clearly
- recording information accurately
- listening actively to enhance understanding of an issue

How will I know if I reach my goals?

As you work through this lesson, tick the 'Achieved' box to show you have achieved your learning goals. If you haven't quite achieved your learning goals, tick 'Not there yet'. Start to think about how you are going to show your learning goals in your challenge. Add an example from your challenge once you have achieved each learning goal.

Lesson 5	Not there yet	Achieved	Example
I can present ideas and information clearly.			
I can record information accurately.			
I can listen actively to enhance my understanding of an issue.			

Prior learning

1 How do you know when someone is listening *actively*? Discuss with a partner.

....

....

....

2 Do your classmates agree? Using what you've learnt from class discussion, add further ideas in a different colour.

The topic I am working on today is …

....

Starter activity

1 Look at the picture your teacher gives you. Describe it to your partner without showing them the picture so that they can sketch it or write notes on what it contains.

Tip

Active listening is about attentively trying to understand what someone says rather than passively hearing the words that someone says.

2 Now it's your turn to listen. Then sketch or write notes about what your partner has described about their picture. On the top of a separate sheet of paper, write the topic of the picture, then give details (in notes or a sketch) below.

3 Did you include all the details in your partner's picture? Yes/No

4 Why do you think this was?

....

5 What did you find challenging about this activity? Why?

....

....

Main activity

1 Watch or listen actively to the video/audio clips your teacher plays. Then complete the table.

Clip	Main message	Other information (e.g. perspective(s); cause(s); consequence(s); course(s) of action)
1		
2		
3		

Tip

When presenting ideas and information, it's important that you speak clearly and slowly and give as many details as you can.

Tip

Show that you are listening actively by giving verbal and non-verbal feedback. This shows you are really interested in what someone is saying.

Tip

Non-verbal feedback includes nodding, leaning forwards and making eye contact.

Tip

Verbal feedback includes affirmations such as 'I see', 'I know', 'Sure' and 'I understand'.

Peer feedback

2 Share your ideas with a partner.
Add further ideas in a different colour.

3 Share your ideas with another pair.
Add further ideas in a different colour.

4 Look at your completed table. Did you find out much information from your classmates? Yes/No

5 How do you think sharing and listening to the ideas of others helps you?

....

Independent reflection activity

How do you know that you've been listening actively?

....

....

What other skills have you used today? How?

....

....

....

Check your learning

If you haven't already done so, complete the **How will I know if I reach my goals?** table with 'Not there yet' or 'Achieved'. Don't forget to add examples from your challenge.

6

Developing communication skills: Lesson 6

5.1 Present coherent, well-reasoned and clearly structured arguments with detailed referencing of sources where appropriate

5.2 Listen to ideas and information and offer well-judged contributions that shape the discussion and enhance understanding of the issue

My learning goals are to develop my knowledge and understanding about:

- presenting ideas and information clearly and with reasoning
- improving listening skills to enhance understanding of an issue

How will I know if I reach my goals?

As you work through this lesson, tick the 'Achieved' box to show you have achieved your learning goals. If you haven't quite achieved your learning goals, tick 'Not there yet'. Start to think about how you are going to show your learning goals in your challenge. Add an example from your challenge once you have achieved each learning goal.

Lesson 6	Not there yet	Achieved	Example
I can present ideas and information clearly and with reasoning.			
I can listen actively to enhance my understanding of an issue.			

Prior learning

Complete the following:

Giving feedback helps ....

....

Receiving feedback helps ....

....

When giving feedback, we should remember ....

....

When receiving feedback, we should remember ....

....

The topic I am working on today is ...

....

Starter activity

Listen to the statements your teacher reads. Write true (T) or false (F) for each statement.

1 .... 6 ....

2 .... 7 ....

3 .... 8 ....

4 .... 9 ....

5 .... 10 ....

Tip

When clarifying information, always check the details are the same on more than one website. This is called cross-referencing.

Main activity

1 Do some research on the statements from the Starter activity. Correct your responses if necessary.

2 Use this table to record evidence to support your responses. For each statement that is false, write a new true statement.

	T/F	Evidence and website address	True statements (if needed)
1			
2			
3			
4			
5			
6			
7			

	T/F	Evidence and website address	True statements (if needed)
8			
9			
10			

3 With a partner, discuss and create five new statements. Ask another pair if the statements are true or false.

	Statements	T/F
11		
12		
13		
14		
15		

Tip

The type of information you find depends on the type of website you use; for example, a blog will give someone's opinion whereas a scientific report will report facts.

Independent reflection activity

I used to think ....

....

Now I think ....

....

This is because ....

....

....

Check your learning

If you haven't already done so, complete the **How will I know if I reach my goals?** table with 'Not there yet' or 'Achieved'. Don't forget to add examples from your challenge.

Self-assessment 2

Look back at self-assessment 1. How much further progress do you feel you have made so far in developing your communication skills?

For each learning objective in the table below, shade in the response that matches yours most closely. Give one example for this response. Eventually, you are aiming for green!

Learning objectives: *to develop my knowledge and understanding about how to …*	RED	AMBER	GREEN
5.1 Present coherent, well-reasoned and clearly structured arguments with detailed referencing of sources where appropriate.	I can write a coherent and clearly structured argument with help. I can write a claim, give reasoning to justify this claim and give evidence to support this claim with help.	I can write a coherent and clearly structured argument. I can write a claim, give reasoning to justify this claim and give evidence to support this claim.	I can write a coherent and clearly structured argument. I can write a claim, give reasoning to justify this claim and give evidence to support this claim. I can help others write coherent and clearly structured arguments.
5.2 Listen to ideas and information and offer well-judged contributions that shape the discussion and enhance understanding of the issue.	I can listen to ideas and information, and note the main points with help. I can give feedback to help improve arguments with help. I can offer suggestions to discussions to enhance my own understanding of an issue.	I can listen to ideas and information, and note the main points. I can give feedback to help improve arguments. I can offer well-judged contributions to discussions to enhance my own understanding of an issue.	I can listen to ideas and information, and note the main points. I can give feedback to help improve arguments. I can offer well-judged contributions to discussions to enhance my own and others' understanding of an issue.

Continued

Examples:

5.1 ....

5.2 ....

Reflect on your responses in your self-assessment and identify two areas for improvement. Set yourself two learning targets – how you will improve upon the two areas. For example, 'I will give feedback to help another team improve the structure of their argument.'

Learning targets:

1 Area for improvement: ....

How I will improve: ....

2 Area for improvement: ....

How I will improve: ....

Challenge topic review

Think about the challenge topic you have been exploring and complete the following statements.

I was surprised to discover that ....

....

I didn't know ....

....

I now think ....

....

7

Getting better at communication skills: Lesson 7

5.1 Present coherent, well-reasoned and clearly structured arguments with detailed referencing of sources where appropriate

5.2 Listen to ideas and information and offer well-judged contributions that shape the discussion and enhance understanding of the issue

My learning goals are to get better at:

- presenting information with reasoning
- sharing relevant ideas with others

How will I know if I reach my goals?

As you work through this lesson, tick the 'Achieved' box to show you have achieved your learning goals. If you haven't quite achieved your learning goals, tick 'Not there yet'. Start to think about how you are going to show your learning goals in your challenge. Add an example from your challenge once you have achieved each learning goal.

Lesson 7	Not there yet	Achieved	Example
I can present information with reasoning.			
I can share relevant ideas and information with others.			

Prior learning

1 What skills have you been developing throughout your Stage 9 Global Perspectives lessons?

....

....

....

....

....

....

2 Share examples with your classmates.

....

....

....

....

....

....

The topic I am working on today is …

....

Tip

When presenting information, use short sentences. Short sentences help people remember the key message.

Starter activity

1 Look at the picture(s) your teacher shows you. Discuss with a partner. Complete the first two columns in the table.

1 What I know about the picture	2 What I want to know about it	3 What I have learnt from research

Class discussion

2 Using what you've learnt from class discussion, add to the first two columns.

3 Do some research to complete the third column.

> **Tip**
>
> As well as presentations and video clips, raps, songs and poems can be creative outcomes to raise awareness about issues.

Main activity

1 As a team, choose just one issue. Using the information from the Starter activity and/or information you have gained about the topic in previous lessons, create an outcome to raise awareness about your chosen issue. The outcome can be a rap, song or poem.

Write your team name at the top of a separate sheet of paper, then write your outcome below. Add references to say where you got your information from.

> **Tip**
>
> When giving feedback, focus on the positive first and then identify something that needs improving or developing.

Peer feedback

2 Share your outcome with your classmates. Decide which teams presented the best three outcomes and why.

1 Team ....

because ....

....

2 Team ....

because ....

....

3 Team ....

because ....

....

Independent reflection activity

Which skill did you improve today?

....

....

How did you improve this skill?

....

....

What skill(s) do you still need to improve?

....

....

Why?

....

....

Check your learning

If you haven't already done so, complete the **How will I know if I reach my goals?** table with 'Not there yet' or 'Achieved'. Don't forget to add examples from your challenge.

Self-assessment 3

Look back at self-assessments 1 and 2. How much further progress do you feel you have made so far in developing your communication skills?

For each learning objective in the table below, shade in the response that matches yours most closely. Give one example for this response. Eventually, you are aiming for green!

Learning objectives: *to get better at understanding how to …*	RED	AMBER	GREEN
5.1 Present coherent, well-reasoned and clearly structured arguments with detailed referencing of sources where appropriate.	I can write a coherent and clearly structured argument with help. I can write a claim, give reasoning to justify this claim and give evidence to support this claim with help. I can reference information sources with help.	I can write a coherent and clearly structured argument. I can write a claim, give reasoning to justify this claim and give evidence to support this claim. I can reference information sources with some accuracy.	I can write a coherent and clearly structured argument. I can write a claim, give reasoning to justify this claim and give evidence to support this claim. I can help others write coherent and clearly structured arguments. I can reference information sources accurately and help others reference information sources.
5.2 Listen to ideas and information and offer well-judged contributions that shape the discussion and enhance understanding of the issue.	I can listen to ideas and information, and note the main points with help. I can give feedback to help improve work with help. I can offer suggestions to discussions to enhance my own understanding of an issue.	I can listen to ideas and information, and note the main points. I can give feedback to help improve work. I can offer well-judged contributions to discussions to enhance my own understanding of an issue.	I can listen to ideas and information, and note the main points. I can give feedback to help improve work. I can offer well-judged contributions to discussions to enhance my own and others' understanding of an issue.

Continued

Examples:

5.1 ....

5.2 ....

Reflect on your responses in your self-assessment and identify two areas for improvement. Set yourself two learning targets – how you will improve upon the two areas. For example, 'When I work with others, I will ask questions if I don't understand what they mean.'

Learning targets:

1 Area for improvement: ....

How I will improve: ....

2 Area for improvement: ....

How I will improve: ....

Challenge topic review

Think about the challenge topic you have been exploring and complete the following statements.

I was surprised to discover that ....

....

I didn't know ....

....

I now think ....

....

> # Section 6
Checkpoint

This section of your Learner's Skills Book 9 helps you to plan, write and review your Checkpoint research report for assessment at the end of Stage 9.

Planning . . .

As you plan your Checkpoint research report, you will write a relevant research question as the title for your report and find sources of information relevant to your research question and to reference in your report. You will conduct research to answer your research question, recording relevant information in your own words. You will also start to develop relevant global and national perspectives, explaining how your chosen global perspective is global in nature and why you have chosen a specific national perspective.

Writing . . .

As you write your Checkpoint research report, you will be using your planning from Lessons 1–3 to write a coherent, well-reasoned and clearly structured individual research report. You will develop and compare global and national perspectives, and explain the causes and consequences of an issue. You will recommend a realistic national or local course of action to help resolve or make a difference to the issue in your research question. You will also evaluate individual sources of information so that you can use your evaluations and reflections on the research conducted and perspectives explored to form your own personal perspective about the issue under investigation.

Reviewing . . .

As you review your Checkpoint research report, you will develop your own personal perspective about the issue in your research question. You will use the mark scheme for the research report to check that you have included all that is required and that your research report is well-structured and coherent. You will add your references in a reference list at the end of your research report and make sure that you have not exceeded the word count of between 800 and 1000 words.

1

Planning your Checkpoint: Lesson 1

1.1 Construct a range of relevant research questions and identify the most appropriate one to follow up

1.2 Identify and accurately reference a wide range of print and multimedia sources and use them to locate relevant information and answer research questions

My learning goals are to plan to:

- write a relevant research question as the title for my Checkpoint research report
- find sources of information to reference in my research report
- do some initial research relevant to my research question

How will I know if I reach my goals?

As you work through this lesson, tick the 'Achieved box' to show you have achieved your learning goals. If you haven't quite achieved your learning goals, tick 'Not there yet' and think about how you are going to achieve them. Add an action point for what you need to do to achieve any of your learning goals.

Lesson 1	Not there yet	Achieved	Action (e.g. look back in my Skills Book for ideas/ support; ask the teacher; do some research at home/ in study time)
I can write a relevant research question as the title for my research report.			
I can find sources of information to reference in my research report.			
I can do some initial research relevant to my research question.			

Prior learning

1 What do you need to remember when formulating a good research question in Global Perspectives? Discuss with a partner.

....

....

....

....

2 Using what you've learnt from class discussion about formulating good research questions, add further ideas in a different colour.

....

....

Starter activity

1 Write down the research questions your teacher gives you. Discuss them with a partner.

A ....

B ....

C ....

D ....

E ....

2 Are these good research questions for Global Perspectives? Why? Why not?

A ....

B ....

C ....

D ....

E ....

Class discussion

3 Do your classmates agree? Change or add to your ideas in a different colour.

Tips

A well-constructed and focused research question is a question that is not too broad, too narrow or too vague. A question that is too broad makes it hard to find a clear answer. One that is too narrow makes it hard to find enough information. One that is too vague makes it difficult to know what to research.

A good research question is relevant to the issue, clear, can be argued and allows for the development of different perspectives and a realistic course of action. It should not be leading or contain bias.

A course of action is something you do to try to help resolve an issue. For example, you might give a presentation to persuade people of the importance of giving hot food to the homeless during the coldest months of the year.

The topic I am working on today is ...

....

Main activity

Complete the following activities on your own. Use the Tips and Section 1 Research in your Skills Book to help you.

1 Formulate a research question about an issue that interests you.

....

....

2 Complete the checklist below. For each response, you need an action point. For example, if you have ticked 'No' for any of the criteria in the checklist, you need to change your research question. If you have ticked 'Not sure', you need to do some initial research to find out if your research question does or does not allow for that particular criteria. If you have ticked 'Yes', you will most likely have a good research question but might check it with your teacher.

Does your research question allow for . . .?	Yes	No	Not sure	**Action** (e.g. initial research on the internet; primary research questionnaire; reword question; ask teacher)
causes and consequences				
claims and reasoning				
relevant supporting evidence				
a clear and explicit global perspective				
a clear and explicit national perspective				

Does your research question allow for . . .?	Yes	No	Not sure	Action (e.g. initial research on the internet; primary research questionnaire; reword question; ask teacher)
a realistic national or local course of action				
an answer that includes your own personal perspective about the issue				
a range of different information sources to include in a reference list				

Self-evaluation

3 After reviewing your completed checklist, change or reword your research question as necessary to make sure you can tick 'Yes' to all the criteria for your new research question. Use a different colour to tick the 'Yes' column on your checklist.

....

....

4 Check your research question with your teacher.
Change or reword your research question if necessary.

....

....

Tips

A claim is an assertion that something is true. A claim in Global Perspectives is followed by one or more reasons for the claim and supported by relevant evidence such as a governmental report or a news story.

A national perspective is the view that a particular country has on an issue. This is usually explained by the laws, policies and/or speeches made by politicians of that country and might be supported by other groups within that country.

Tips

A global perspective is a view on an issue that either has global influence or takes account of the nature of the issue globally. An example of a global perspective could come from the United Nations as it is an international agency with global influence.

A personal perspective is the view that a person has on an issue after exploring different perspectives and information sources and reflecting on the research conducted about the issue.

A reference list is a list of all the sources of information you have researched and used in your own work. A reference list should include the author, date published, title, and publication or website address, and if a website address, the date accessed.

Asking other people questions is called primary research and primary research enables the researcher to gain first-hand accounts of events or opinions about issues.

Secondary research comes from secondary sources of information, such as the internet or books. These sources of information are created later by someone who did not experience an event first-hand or is reporting someone else's viewpoint or opinion.

Independent reflection activity

What skill(s) did you use today?

....

....

How?

....

....

Check your learning

If you haven't already done so, complete the **How will I know if I reach my goals?** table with 'Not there yet' or 'Achieved'. Don't forget to add examples from your challenge.

2

Planning your Checkpoint: Lesson 2

1.3 Select most suitable methods and conduct research to test predictions and answer a research question

1.4 Select, organise and effectively record relevant information from a wide range of sources and findings from research, justifying the method chosen

My learning goals are to plan to:

- conduct research to answer my research question
- record relevant information in my own words

How will I know if I reach my goals?

As you work through this lesson, tick the 'Achieved box' to show you have achieved your learning goals. If you haven't quite achieved your learning goals, tick 'Not there yet' and think about how you are going to meet them. Add an action point for what you need to do to achieve any of your learning goals.

Lesson 2	Not there yet	Achieved	Action (e.g. look back in my Skills Book for ideas/support; ask the teacher; do some research at home/in study time)
I can conduct research to answer my research question.			
I can record relevant information in my own words.			

The topic I am working on today is ...

....

Prior learning

1 Write down your research question from last lesson.

....

....

2 Complete the table, making note of any relevant information sources you already have (e.g. text about the causes of climate change; website about UN Sustainable Development Goal 2; video clip about the effects of poverty).

Criteria	Information sources
Causes	
Consequences	
Global perspective	
National perspective	
Course(s) of action (national/local)	

Starter activity

1 Look at your completed table from your Prior learning.
What further information do you need to be able to answer your research question?

....

....

....

....

2 Might you need to do some primary research? Yes/No

Why? ....

....

Main activity

Use your research question. Find further information sources for each of the criteria in the table and make notes in your own words. Add the reference for each information source.

Criteria	Reference (remember to include all the necessary information)	Notes (to help you write about the necessary criteria)
Causes		
Consequences		
Global perspective		
National perspective		
Course(s) of action		

Tips

To make notes, you need to skim the text to find what you are looking for (e.g. causes), then read the text, make sense of it and write notes in your own words.

A reference list is a list of all the sources of information you have researched and used in your own work.

When writing a reference, you need to include the title of the article, the date, the author and the name of the publisher. If the source is online, you also include the website address and the date you accessed the source.

If the name of a website ends with .gov and then a country abbreviation (e.g. .uk, .qa or .my), it is probably a reliable government website.

If the website ends in .org, it is probably the website of a non-profit organisation. These websites are good information sources but are probably biased.

If the website address has 'wiki' in it, be careful, as wiki and social media websites can be edited by anyone so the information might not be true. Always cross-reference information obtained from this type of website.

Independent reflection activity

What skill(s) did you use or improve today?

....

....

How?

....

....

Check your learning

If you haven't already done so, complete the **How will I know if I reach my goals?** table with 'Not there yet' or 'Achieved'. Don't forget to add examples from your challenge.

3

Planning your Checkpoint: Lesson 3

2.1 Identify perspectives and synthesise arguments and evidence from a range of sources on a given topic

2.2 Identify patterns and trends in graphical or numerical data in order to support an argument

My learning goals are to plan to:

- begin developing a global perspective by synthesising arguments and evidence
- begin developing a national perspective by synthesising arguments and evidence
- start comparing global and national perspectives

How will I know if I reach my goals?

As you work through this lesson, tick the 'Achieved box' to show you have achieved your learning goals. If you haven't quite achieved your learning goals, tick 'Not there yet' and think about how you are going to meet them. Add an action point for what you need to do to achieve any of your learning goals.

Lesson 3	Not there yet	Achieved	Action (e.g. look back in my Skills Book for ideas/ support; ask the teacher; do some research at home/ in study time)
I am beginning to develop a global perspective by synthesising arguments and evidence.			
I am beginning to develop a national perspective by synthesising arguments and evidence.			
I am starting to compare the global and national perspectives.			

Prior learning

1 Give an example for each of the following.

Global perspective: ....

National perspective: ....

2 Explain why your examples in task **1** are global and national perspectives.

Global perspective: ....

National perspective: ....

3 After class discussion about global and national perspectives, make any changes to your responses in task **2**.

The topic I am working on today is …

....

Starter activity

1 Review the notes for your global and national perspectives from the Main activity in Lesson 2.

2 Add any further ideas from your research (perhaps from your Prior learning or independent study to develop your global and national perspective).

....

....

....

Main activity

1 Draft two paragraphs for each of the perspectives for your Checkpoint. Add a further paragraph of three or four sentences to compare/contrast your global and national perspectives.

Research question:	
Global perspective	1
	2
National perspective	1
	2
Comparison	

Tips

When introducing different perspectives, use transition words/phrases such as 'according to'; 'think that'; 'is of the opinion that'; 'believe that'; 'view this situation as'.

When developing perspectives, avoid just giving information about different countries. However, you can later use examples from different countries to support your perspectives. For example, 'Fishermen in Malaysia are concerned that they will lose their livelihoods if fish stocks run out' is an example of what a group of people think and can support a perspective.

When referring to evidence to support perspectives, use transition words/phrases such as 'for example'; 'for instance'; 'to demonstrate'.

You should start a new paragraph for each perspective.

To compare perspectives, use transition words/phrases such as 'on the other hand'; 'in contrast to'; 'in comparison'; 'however'; 'whilst'; 'whereas'; rather than'.

Self-evaluation

2 Review your draft paragraphs and make any amendments necessary.

3 Check your draft paragraphs by completing the table.

Research question:			
Have you . . .?	**Yes**	**No**	**Notes** (e.g. need further evidence; add more transition words to compare perspectives; explain why I chose my national perspective)
developed a global perspective			
developed a national perspective			
explained why your global perspective is global			
explained why your national perspective is national			
explained why you have chosen this national perspective			

Have you . . .?	Yes	No	Notes (e.g. need further evidence; add more transition words to compare perspectives; explain why I chose my national perspective)
given three pieces of evidence to support your global perspective			
given three pieces of evidence to support your national perspective			
compared your global and national perspective			
used transition words/ phrases (e.g. 'however', 'on the other hand') to compare your global and national perspectives			

Independent reflection activity

1 Look at your draft paragraphs from the Main activity. What did you think about the issue in your research question before you developed your global and national perspectives?

....

....

....

....

2 After consideration of your global and national perspectives, what do you now think about the issue in your research question?

....

....

....

....

Continued

3 Has your personal perspective about the issue in your research question developed or changed? Yes/No

How and why?

....

....

....

....

Check your learning

If you haven't already done so, complete the **How will I know if I reach my goals?** table with 'Not there yet' or 'Achieved'. Don't forget to add action points if necessary.

Checklist 1

Look at Checklist 1. How much progress have you made?

Review your planning for your draft Checkpoint by completing the table below. For each of the criteria, tick 'YES' or 'NO'. Where you have ticked 'NO', add at least one action point. Eventually, you are aiming for 'YES' for each of the criteria.

CRITERIA *I have…*	Yes	No	ACTION POINT (e.g. Make my global perspective clearer and more explicit; explain causes more fully; add transition words for comparing global and national perspectives)
formulated a focused research question			
explained relevant causes and consequences			
included relevant information from different sources			

Continued

CRITERIA *I have...*	Yes	No	ACTION POINT (e.g. Make my global perspective clearer and more explicit; explain causes more fully; add transition words for comparing global and national perspectives)
presented a clear and explicit global perspective			
presented a clear and explicit national perspective			
compared global and national perspectives			
proposed a realistic national/local course of action			
reflected on how my personal perspective has developed/changed			

Next steps

Reflect on your responses to Checklist 1. Summarise what you need to do before you are ready to write the next draft of your Checkpoint research report.

I need to ....

....

....

....

Writing your Checkpoint: Lesson 4

2.1 Identify perspectives and synthesise arguments and evidence from a range of sources on a given topic

2.3 Make some links between causes and consequences of an issue at personal, local and global levels

5.1 Present coherent, well-reasoned and clearly structured arguments with detailed referencing of sources where appropriate

My learning goals are to write:

- a full global and a full national perspective, and a comparison of these
- the causes and consequences of the issue
- clear notes on any source material I have used

How will I know if I reach my goals?

As you work through this lesson, tick the 'Achieved box' to show you have achieved your learning goals. If you haven't quite achieved your learning goals, tick 'Not there yet' and think about how you are going to meet them. Add an action point for what you need to do to achieve any of your learning goals.

Lesson 4	Not there yet	Achieved	Action (e.g. look back in my Skills Book for ideas/ support; ask the teacher; do some research at home/ in study time)
I can write a full global and a full national perspective, and a comparison of these.			
I can explain the causes and consequences of an issue.			
I can write clear notes on any source material I have used.			

Prior learning

1 What words/phrases are useful for comparing global and national perspectives? Discuss with a partner.

....

....

2 Using what you have learnt from class discussion, add any further words/phrases for comparing global and national perspectives.

....

....

The topic I am working on today is ...

....

Starter activity

1 Look at your draft paragraph comparing your global and national perspectives from Lesson 3. Add words/phrases to show the similarities and differences between the perspectives.
Write the revised paragraph on a separate sheet of paper.

Self-evaluation

2 Highlight the words/phrases that compare your global and national perspectives.

3 Are the differences and similarities between the global and national perspective clear? Yes/No

4 If you answered 'No' in task 3, make your comparisons clearer.

Main activity

1 a Write down some words/phrases that signal causes.

....

....

b Write down some words/phrases that signal consequences.

....

....

Class discussion

2 After class discussion about words/phrases that signal causes and consequences, add to your lists in task 1 in a different colour.

3 On your own, using your own research question and notes from Lesson 2, write a paragraph or two to explain the causes and consequences of the issue in your research question.

Causes	1
	2
Consequences	1
	2

Self-evaluation

4 Look at the paragraphs you wrote in task 3. Answer the following questions. Give examples.

1 Are the causes of the issue clear? Yes/No

Example: ....

2 Have you included appropriate signal words for the causes? Yes/No

Example: ....

3 Have you explained the causes of the issue rather than simply stated what they are? Yes/No

Example: ....

4 Have you included reference to information sources to support your explanation of the causes of the issue? Yes/No

Example: ....

5 Are the consequences of the issue clear? Yes/No

Example: ....

6 Have you included appropriate signal words for the consequences? Yes/No

Example: ....

7 Have you explained the consequences of the issue rather than simply stated what they are? Yes/No

Example: ....

8 Have you included reference to information sources to support your explanation of the consequences of the issue? Yes/No

Example: ....

5 If you have answered 'No' to any of the questions in task 4, make changes to your paragraph(s).

Tips

When discussing the causes and consequences of something at a personal level, consider the question, 'What does it mean to me?'

When discussing the causes and consequences of something at a local level, consider the question, 'What does it mean to my community?'

When discussing the causes and consequences of something at a global level, consider the question, 'What does it mean to the world?'

To explain a cause or consequence, state what the cause or consequence is and then add supporting details. For example: 'A cause of ocean pollution is the amount of plastic that ends up in the oceans after being thrown away by humans. For example, according to a report in a scientific journal (Brown, 2015), between approximately 5 and 12 million tonnes of plastic end up in the ocean every year.'

Independent reflection activity

Do you think that you can now explain the causes and consequences of your issue (in your research question)?

....

....

If you answered 'No', what do you need to do to improve your understanding?

....

....

Check your learning

If you haven't already done so, complete the **How will I know if I reach my goals?** table with 'Not there yet' or 'Achieved'. Don't forget to add action points if necessary.

5

Writing your Checkpoint: Lesson 5

2.4 Recommend an appropriate course of action and explain possible consequences for a national or global issue

5.1 Present coherent, well-reasoned and clearly structured arguments with detailed referencing of sources where appropriate

My learning goals are to write:

- an appropriate and realistic national/local course of action, explaining how it will help to resolve an issue
- clear notes on any source material I have used

How will I know if I reach my goals?

As you work through this lesson, tick the 'Achieved box' to show you have achieved your learning goals. If you haven't quite achieved your learning goals, tick 'Not there yet' and think about how you are going to meet them. Add an action point for what you need to do to achieve any of your learning goals.

Lesson 5	Not there yet	Achieved	Action (e.g. look back in my Skills Book for ideas/support; ask the teacher; do some research at home/in study time)
I can propose an appropriate and realistic national/local course of action and explain how it will help resolve an issue.			
I can write clear notes on any source material I have used.			

Prior learning

1 What do you think is meant by 'an appropriate and realistic course of action' in Global Perspectives? Discuss with a partner.

....

....

2 Give some examples of courses of action for an issue.

....

....

....

3 Using what you've learnt from class discussion, add further examples of courses of action to your list in task 2.

The topic I am working on today is ...

....

Starter activity

1 On a separate sheet of paper, write out the notes you made in Lesson 2 for possible courses of action to help resolve or make a positive difference to the issue in your research question. Make any changes in a different colour.

2 Review the paragraphs you wrote in Lessons 2 and 4 for the causes and consequences of the issue in your research question and the global and national perspectives. Add further ideas for a course(s) of action to help resolve or make a positive difference to the issue in your research question.

Tips

A course of action is something you can do to help make a positive difference to an issue. Courses of action need to be realistic; for example, raising awareness about an issue so that people might change their own behaviour.

When considering actions to help resolve issues, ask yourself: 'What is the issue?'; 'Why is the issue important?'; 'Who does the issue affect?'; 'When is action needed?'; 'Which resources do I need to take action?'; 'How will I know if my action is effective?'

Main activity

1 On your own, using your notes from the Starter activity, write a paragraph explaining your proposed course(s) of action to help resolve or make a difference to the issue in your research question. Write on a separate sheet of paper.

Self-evaluation

2 Have you explained how your course(s) of action might work to help resolve or make a positive difference to your issue? Yes/No

3 If you answered 'No' to task 2, amend your paragraph in task 1 so that it includes not only your course(s) of action but also how it/they might work to help resolve or make a positive difference to your issue.

Tips

You need to explain how your course of action is going to resolve or make a difference to an issue; for example, by giving an example of where it is working somewhere else.

There may be many different actions that can help make a positive difference to an issue. Choose one most suitable for the issue.

Independent reflection activity

1 Are you happy that your course(s) of action is/are realistic and can help resolve or make a positive difference to the issue in your research question? Yes/No

2 If you answered 'No', what do you now need to do to be able to answer 'Yes'?

....

....

....

Check your learning

If you haven't already done so, complete the **How will I know if I reach my goals?** table with 'Not there yet' or 'Achieved'. Don't forget to add action points if necessary.

6

Writing your Checkpoint: Lesson 6

1.2 Identify and accurately reference a wide range of print and multimedia sources and use them to locate relevant information and answer research questions

3.1 Evaluate a range of sources, considering the author and purpose and how well they are supported by other sources, explaining why some may be biased

My learning goals are to write:

- accurate references for the information sources used in my Checkpoint research report
- an evaluation of an individual source of information

How will I know if I reach my goals?

As you work through this lesson, tick the 'Achieved box' to show you have achieved your learning goals. If you haven't quite achieved your learning goals, tick 'Not there yet' and think about how you are going to meet them. Add an action point for what you need to do to achieve any of your learning goals.

Lesson 6	Not there yet	Achieved	Action (e.g. look back in my Skills Book for ideas/ support; ask the teacher; do some research at home/ in study time)
I can write an accurate reference for an individual source of information.			
I can evaluate an individual source of information and explain why it might contain bias.			

Prior learning

1 What do you think it means to evaluate a source of information in Global Perspectives? Discuss with your partner.

....

....

....

2 After class discussion, do your classmates have any further ideas?

....

....

....

The topic I am working on today is …

....

Starter activity

1 Look back at the sources of information you used whilst planning your Checkpoint assessment in Lesson 2. Write out three of your references here.

1 ....

2 ....

3 ....

Tip

When writing a reference, you need to include the title of the article, the date, the author and the name of the publisher. If the source is online, then you also include the website address and the date you accessed the source.

Self-evaluation

2 Check that your references in task 1 are complete and accurate. Complete the table using three different colours, one for each reference listed in task 1.

Website address	Yes	No
author		
date		
title of the article		
the website address (if appropriate)		
the date accessed (if a website)		

3 If you have any ticks in the 'No' column, amend the reference and write it out again.

....

....

....

Main activity

1 Evaluate each of the three information sources in your reference list in the Starter activity. Complete one checklist for each information source.

Source 1: ....

Checklist	Yes/ No	**Notes** (e.g. type of evidence; who wrote/ published the source; any bias?)
Are the arguments in the information source supported by evidence?		
Have you heard of the author/ organisation that published the information source?		
Does the information source look real?		
Is the evidence to support the arguments strong?		
Does the information source sound believable?		
Is the author of the information source a real person?		
Is there anything odd about the date when the information source was published?		
Is the information presented free from bias?		
Are there any errors in spelling or grammar (in text only)?		
Is the story presented in a coherent and logical way?		

Source 2: ....

Checklist	Yes/ No	Notes (e.g. type of evidence; who wrote/ published the source; any bias?)
Are the arguments in the information source supported by evidence?		
Have you heard of the author/ organisation that published the information source?		
Does the information source look real?		
Is the evidence to support the arguments strong?		
Does the information source sound believable?		
Is the author of the information source a real person?		
Is there anything odd about the date when the information source was published?		
Is the information presented free from bias?		
Are there any errors in spelling or grammar (in text only)?		
Is the story presented in a coherent and logical way?		

Source 3: ....

Checklist	Yes/ No	**Notes** (e.g. type of evidence; who wrote/ published the source; any bias?)
Are the arguments in the information source supported by evidence?		
Have you heard of the author/ organisation that published the information source?		
Does the information source look real?		
Is the evidence to support the arguments strong?		
Does the information source sound believable?		
Is the author of the information source a real person?		
Is there anything odd about the date when the information source was published?		
Is the information presented free from bias?		
Are there any errors in spelling or grammar (in text only)?		
Is the story presented in a coherent and logical way?		

2 Choose one of your references from task 1. Write a paragraph of two or three sentences to evaluate this source of information.

....

....

....

....

Tips

To evaluate a source, you need to give its strengths and weaknesses.

Tips

A reliable source is one that provides a detailed, well-reasoned argument, analysis or discussion that is supported by strong evidence.

It is most likely that you will have heard of the more reliable sources of information that provide strong evidence, for example, newspapers like *The Guardian*, *The Huffington Post* and *The Times of India*, news agencies like the BBC, CNN and Al Jazeera, and global organisations such as the United Nations and the WWF (World Wide Fund for Nature).

To check a source is reliable, check the author, the date and the evidence presented in support of the argument(s).

To check a source for bias, look to see if the information presented is one-sided or focused only on the author's opinion.

A biased author may not present all the facts or develop a reasoned argument to support their opinion(s). For example, someone in favour of technological advancement is unlikely to give the disadvantages of digital technologies.

An effective information source has a logical argument that makes sense and is supported with reasoning and evidence. To judge if an information source is effective, you need to be persuaded by the argument(s) it makes.

Evidence is anything that can support or back up a claim; for example, a scientific report, a study or a quotation from someone or something that someone has read.

Independent reflection activity

1 Do you feel confident that you can evaluate an individual source of information? Yes/No

2 If you answered, 'No' in task 1, what do you need to do to increase your confidence?

....

....

Check your learning

If you haven't already done so, complete the **How will I know if I reach my goals?** table with 'Not there yet' or 'Achieved'. Don't forget to add action points if necessary.

Checklist 2

Look back at Checklist 1. How much further progress have you made?

Review your draft Checkpoint by completing the table below. For each of the criteria, tick 'YES' or 'NO'. Where you have ticked 'NO', add at least one action point. Eventually, you are aiming for 'YES' for each of the criteria.

CRITERIA *I have…*	Yes	No	ACTION POINT (e.g. Make my global perspective clearer and more explicit; explain causes more fully; add transition words for comparing global and national perspectives)
formulated a focused research question			
explained relevant causes and consequences			
evaluated individual sources of information			
included relevant information from different sources			
presented a clear and explicit global perspective			
presented a clear and explicit national perspective			
compared global and national perspectives			
proposed a realistic national/local course of action			
reflected on how my personal perspective has developed/changed			
presented the content in a well-structured and coherent way			
referenced information sources in a consistently accurate way			

Next steps

Reflect on your responses to Checklist 2. Summarise what you need to do before you are ready to write the next draft of your Checkpoint research report.

I need to ....

....

....

....

Reviewing your Checkpoint: Lesson 7

1.1 Construct a range of relevant research questions and identify the most appropriate one to follow up

4.3 Explain how personal perspective on an issue has changed as a result of conducting research and exploring different perspectives

5.1 Present coherent, well-reasoned and clearly structured arguments with detailed referencing of sources where appropriate

My learning goals are to review:

- the research question, checking its relevance with the chosen issue and rest of the research report
- my personal perspective and explain how it has developed or changed as a result of research conducted and perspectives explored
- the research report, checking its structure and coherence

How will I know if I reach my goals?

As you work through this lesson, tick the 'Achieved box' to show you have achieved your learning goals. If you haven't quite achieved your learning goals, tick 'Not there yet' and think about how you are going to meet them. Add an action point for what you need to do to achieve any of your learning goals.

Lesson 7	Not there yet	Achieved	Action (e.g. look back in my Skills Book for ideas/ support; ask the teacher; do some research at home/ in study time)
I can check the relevance of my research question to my chosen issue and the rest of my research report.			
I can explain how my personal perspective has developed/changed.			
I can check the structure and coherence of my research report.			

Prior learning

1 Think back over your Global Perspectives lessons. What do you think you need to be able to do to explain your own personal perspective in Global Perspectives? Discuss with a partner.

....

....

....

2 After class discussion, do your classmates have any further ideas?

....

....

....

The topic I am working on today is …

....

Starter activity

1 Review the work you have done for your Checkpoint assessment. On your own, answer the following questions:

a What did you think about your issue before you started your research?

....

....

b What do you think about your issue now?

....

....

c Has your personal viewpoint about the issue developed or changed? Explain how.

....

....

d Why do you think this is?

....

....

Tip

When developing your own personal perspective on an issue, think about the information you found interesting and why this was, and how this information might have influenced your own thoughts about the issue.

Tip

The ideas, experiences and perspectives of others all influence your own personal perspective.

Tips

You can change your personal perspective as a result of research into the causes and consequences of an issue and exploring the different perspectives on an issue.

To explain your own personal perspective, ask yourself, 'What did I used to think?'; 'What do I think now?'; and 'How and why has my thinking developed or changed?'

Main activity

1 Use your research question and the rest of your Checkpoint assessment (paragraphs about causes and consequences of the issue, global and national perspectives; course(s) of action; evaluation of individual information sources) together with the notes you made in the Starter activity.

Write a paragraph to explain your own personal perspective about your issue and how it has developed and changed, and why.

....

....

....

....

....

....

Self-evaluation

2 Re-read your paragraph from task **1**. Have you:

- **a** Said what you used to think about the issue? Yes/No
- **b** Said if your viewpoint has developed or changed? Yes/No
- **c** Said why your viewpoint has developed or changed? Yes/No
- **d** Used evidence to support your new viewpoint? Yes/No

3 If you answered 'No' to any of the questions in task **2**, amend your responses in task **1** so that you can respond 'Yes' to all the questions.

4 **a** Add your personal perspective paragraph to the rest of your research report.

- **b** Add a sentence or two to introduce your research.
- **c** Make sure you have answered your research question in your conclusion.
- **d** Check the word count of your research report is less than 1000 words in total (without the reference list), adding or deleting words as appropriate.

e Write out your research report in full.
You should do this on a computer.

f Add your reference list to your research report.

Independent reflection activity

What skill(s) have you further developed this lesson?

....

Give an example of how you have developed this skill further?
You can give more than one example if you have developed more than one skill.

....

....

Check your learning

If you haven't already done so, complete the **How will I know if I reach my goals?** table with 'Not there yet' or 'Achieved'. Don't forget to add action points if necessary.

Checklist 3

Look back at Checklist 2. How much further progress have you made?

Review your final draft of your Checkpoint by completing the table below. For each of the criteria, tick 'YES' or 'NO'. Where you have ticked 'NO,' add at least one action point. Eventually, you are aiming for 'YES' for each of the criteria.

CRITERIA *I have…*	Yes	No	ACTION POINT (e.g. Make my global perspective clearer and more explicit; explain causes more fully; add transition words for comparing global and national perspectives, evaluate another information source)
formulated a focused research question			
explained relevant causes and consequences			

Continued

evaluated individual sources of information			
included relevant information from different sources			
presented a clear and explicit global perspective			
presented a clear and explicit national perspective			
compared global and national perspectives			
proposed a realistic national/local course of action			
reflected on how personal perspective has developed/changed			
presented the content in a well-structured and coherent way			
referenced information sources in a consistently accurate way			

Next steps

Reflect on your responses to Checklist 3. Summarise what you need to do before you are ready to write the final copy of your Checkpoint research report.

I need to ....

....

....

....

Glossary

active listening	attentively trying to understand what someone says rather than passively hearing the words
analysis	detailed examination of something, breaking it down into different parts, often causes and consequences of an issue for Global Perspectives
area for development	something to improve on
argument	consists of a claim, the reason(s) for that claim and the evidence to support the claim
bias	a judgement based on a personal point of view, which may be unfair or could favour or be prejudiced against a certain side
cause	the reason(s) why an event or situation happens
cite	to refer to a text, book or author as evidence to help support an argument
claim	a statement or an assertion that something IS true
coherent	a text that makes sense through the organisation of its content
collaboration	working together with others
communication	a way to transfer information from one place to another, usually by speaking and writing
consequence	the result or effect of something that has happened
counterargument	a reason or set of reasons that oppose/go against an idea presented in an argument
course of action	something you do to try to help resolve, or make a positive difference to, an issue
cross-referencing	checking details are the same in more than one information source
double-bar graph	a bar graph that compares two sets of data
evaluation	identifying strengths and limitations/weaknesses
evidence	the available facts or information showing the truth of an argument
fact	something that can be proven to be true
fake news	false information deliberately created to trick people into believing it is true
feedback	giving information to someone about something to help them develop or improve
global perspective	thinking about a situation or issue as it relates to the whole world
limitation	usually something that is lacking or not done very well, or is restrictive somehow
national perspective	thinking about a situation or issue as it relates to a specific country
non-verbal feedback	feedback that is not spoken, including nodding, leaning forwards and making eye contact
opinion	a viewpoint/idea; cannot be proven
paragraph	section of writing in the main body of a text that usually presents a claim, reasoning and evidence

personal perspective	what an individual thinks about a topic/issue, supported by evidence
personal strength	something an individual is good at
perspective	a certain world view or way of looking at an issue
prediction	a statement about what might happen in the future or what might be the cause or consequence of something that has already happened
primary research	the method for collecting data that has not been collected before and is collected directly from individuals, groups of people or research observations
reference	details of a source of information, including the author, title, publication date, any website address and date the website was accessed
reference list	a list of all the sources of information researched and used in written work
reflection	to think hard about something
reflective learning	to think hard about what you are learning
reliable source of information	a source that can be trusted to be true
research	a way of collecting information
research question	a question that enables you to carry out research about a specific issue
secondary research	the method of collecting data from existing/published sources of information
shared outcome	something produced as a team
stakeholder	someone with a vested interested in a topic/issue
synthesise	to bring together ideas from different sources to present an argument or develop a perspective in one's own words
teamwork	working with a group of people towards a shared outcome
text structure	how the text is organised so that the reader can follow it
topic-specific words	words that are related to a main idea/topic
transition words	words that help to link ideas together, for example, 'Finally', 'As you can see'
unreliable source	a source that cannot be trusted to be true
verbal feedback	spoken feedback, including affirmations such as 'I see', 'I know', 'Sure' and 'I understand'

› Acknowledgements

The authors and publishers acknowledge the following sources of copyright material and are grateful for the permissions granted. While every effort has been made, it has not always been possible to identify the sources of all the material used, or to trace all copyright holders. If any omissions are brought to our notice, we will be happy to include the appropriate acknowledgements on reprinting.

Thanks to the following for permission to reproduce images:

Cover: yanikap/Getty Images

Inside: FatCamera/GI; Imaginima/GI; SDI Productions/GI; Eli_asenova/GI; D76MasahiroIKEDA/GI; SolStock/GI; Klaus Vedfelt/GI; Roberto Schmidt/GI; Indranil Mukherjee/GI; Monkeybusinessimages/GI; Kentaroo Tryman/GI; SolStock/GI; track5/GI; SolStock/GI; fizkes/GI; Photo and Co/GI; miodrag ignjatovic/GI; SAEED KHAN/GI; vladj55/GI; Icon Sportswire/GI; SolStock/GI; Bradley Kanaris/GI; NurPhoto/GI; Pakin Songmor/GI; SOPA Images/GI; Image Source/GI; Ullstein bild/GI; Yuliang11/GI; Westend61/GI; Michael Mhleck/GI; Hyoung Chang/GI; Mario Tama/GI; Peter Muller/GI; Vgajic/GI; MediaNews Group/GI; Tim Graham/GI; Stefano Montesi/GI; Rebecca Sapp/GI; Boston Globe/GI; Drew Angerer/GI; DMEPhotography/GI; Colin McPherson/GI; Mitchell Leff/GI; Christian Science Monitor/GI; Ascent Xmedia/GI; ARUN SANKAR/GI; Education Images/GI; EuropaNewswire/GI; KONTROLAB/GI; Stefano Montesi/GI; CHANDAN KHANNA/GI; XAVIER GALIANA/GI; AIZAR RALDES/GI; GI/Westend61; Stefano Montesi/GI; David Butow/GI; Artur Lebedev/GI; Philippe TURPIN/GI; Mel Melcon/GI; POJCHEEWIN YAPRASERT PHOTOGRAPHY/GI; ColorBlind Images/GI

Key: GI= Getty Images